GUIDE DOG
WOODY

and the

Blind Chick

SUE-ELLEN LOVETT

Woody has changed my life.

Without him, I wouldn't be able to get out to the stable every day and ride my horses.

He's a cheeky monkey – and my best mate.

@MegRose Photography

OTHER GREAT ADVENTURES BY SUE-ELLEN LOVETT

Johno and the Blind Chick
Vision is More than Seeing (Book 1)

Johno & The Blind Chick
Walk in My Shoes (Book 2)

Guide Dog Woody & The Blind Chick
One Step at a Time (Book 3)

The Blind Chick
Vision is Much More than Seeing (Autobiography)

Documentary on Sue-Ellen Lovett
– Overcoming Adversity & Moving Forward (out soon)

*

To get your hands on any, or all, of these
brilliant adventures, simply go to:

www.TheBlindChick.com.au

*

What People Are Saying...

"I don't qualify for a Guide Dog but after reading this book I am forever changed. Woody's guiding light shone right into my heart. I couldn't put it down.

I thought I knew what it takes to be a Guide Dog but until now I really had no idea. I'm going to contact Guide Dogs and get involved. I'm hooked!

Thank you, thank you Guide Dog Woody and the Blind Chick."

Ann Mcleod

"Some books are like droplets on a window, the memory of them is there one minute, gone the next. Not memorable at all. Buckle up! One read of Woody's hilarious and very real adventure into the incredibly life changing world of guiding, isn't enough. I'm on my third read.

Please tell me there's a movie in the pipeline."

J.A. Thompson

"Thank you Woody, for the rollicking great read and thank you Sheila Woodcock, the long term supporter of Guide Dogs whose years of donations created multiple Woody's for so many worthy people.

I aspire to be like Sheila. While I may not be able to donate as much as her, I'll certainly give it a good hot crack."

Jackie Boorne

*

Row one: Donna, Tara, Eccles & Jag (@2CPhotography).
Row two: Prada (@Noni McCarthy), Amani (@kathy Hyde, Dubbo) & Woody

To all the Guide Dogs that have come before me, Donna, Tara, Eccles, Jag, Prada and Amani. I don't just know your names. I know your funny ways, the many adventures you safely guided my Blind Chick on, not just around the house or the farm, but around the world! On planes, trains, buses and in cars you never waivered.

The Blind Chick talks of you, you may be gone, but you're never forgotten.

Throughout each of my days from when I'm first greeted by her happy "Good morning gorgeous" to when I hear her breathing slow into slumberland, I will give her the best me I can be. I will be you... with extras!

To my namesake Mrs Woodcock, thank you for your generous donation to Guide Dogs.

Your friend

Woody

Guide Dog Extraordinaire

*

PREFACE

Well, I must say I was quite humbled and honoured when Woody approached me to write this book's preface. I realise this is generally done by the author, but he says I am such a great observer, with everything that has happened since he came into the Blind Chick's life, so here goes.

It was a day that started like many others, sunny, birds chirping, wind blowing branches gently in a slight breeze, but it certainly didn't end that way. I'll never forget the day a very big yellow, well maybe golden, dog arrived here. He had long legs, big paws and a very waggly tail!

Well, he wasn't here long before they put this harness thing on him and instantly it became apparent that this dog with the long legs and waggly tail was going to be guiding the Blind Chickie babe around. This was all pretty exciting.

The lady that arrived to deliver the big golden dog, her name is Danni, she's a Guide Dog Trainer, she and the Blind Chick started training with the dog. Oh, by the way, the big waggly dog is called Woody. He was being taught a few short destinations. By destinations I mean places he needs to learn that our Blind Chick goes to regularly, like: "Arena", or "Round Yard". He did that very well, with much care and confidence.

Now I must point out to you that this big yellow golden dog is called a Labrador and he as a Guide Dog has oodles of confidence. I mean oodles and oodles of confidence.

I have to admit that at first, his size and his exuberance and his very big waggly tail sounded like he was demolishing the house, it really frightened me. I truly wasn't sure whether he was going to chase me, maybe eat me, or both! But as time has gone on, we've become mates. And boy oh boy he's such a wonderful Guide Dog. He does his job of being our Blind Chick's guide, brilliantly.

It was also quite special watching Woody meet Lola, the Blind Chick's horse for the first time. Lola's nose was very out of joint because Woody was getting treats and she wasn't! But the Blind Chick quickly fixed that, she now has a bum bag with Woody treats and a bum bag with Lola treats in it. They're both very happy little campers.

During his training here Woody has had to learn many new destinations, like "find Lola," "find Tack Shed", "go to the Dressage Arena." As soon as the Blind Chick says any of those words, off he goes guiding her where she needs to go.

I watch them do this special tango each day. The Blind Chick gives him the destination, "Find Lola" and off he goes, guiding her into the paddock where Lola is standing quietly. After the Blind Chick has put Lola's head collar and lead rope on, she asks Woody "find Tack Shed" and off they go.

When they get to the Tack Shed the Blind Chick saddles Lola then Woody guides them to the Dressage Arena, "find Dressage Arena". How cool is that! I think it rocks, especially when you think he's just a dog. But not just any ordinary dog, Woody is a very clever dog.

As I write this it's now been a wonderful seven months watching the growth and the confidence of Woody, the Blind Chick and Lola. What a difference this wonderful Guide Dog has made to the Blind Chick's life.

Best of all for me is Mr Long Legs with the waggly tail hasn't managed to take my position in the family. That being me firmly ensconced between Matthew and the Blind Chick when they sleep! They affectionately call me the contraceptive cat. I'm very handsome and I know I am loved very much.

Our Blind Chick has a favourite saying – "Just one step at a time."

So, let's take that first step together. Turn the page and come on a journey with Woody, the amazing Guide Dog, our Blind Chick and her horses.

It's purrrrfect, you're going to love it.

Thunder Paws

*

Contents

*

Stay up to date with Sue-Ellen's
adventures via her Facebook:

www.facebook.com/JohnoAndTheBlindChick

&

www.facebook.com/SueEllen.Lovett

*

I am Australian

Written by: Guide Dog Woody about his life with Sue-Ellen Lovett
Copyright: Sue-Ellen Lovett

@MegRose Photography

I am the Dreamtime.
The keeper of the flame.
My golden eyes become hers.
Independence, mobility, and freedom
arrive with me.
Her confidence returns.
I am Australian.

She may be blind to others;
she is not blind to me.
For I have found her secret,
that my Blind Chick can see.
Though eyesight may elude her,
I have known it from the start,
She doesn't need eyes;
Sue sees with her heart.

Her sense of hearing, smell and touch,
are sharpened by her plight,
Her kind deeds and compassion
have kept her from the night.
And no complaints are offered,
affliction is her shield,
I am her knight in shining armour,
upon life's battlefield.
I am, we are, Australian.

They call me a Guide Dog,
But I'm so much more than that.
I guide, I encourage, I protect.
I am friend, companion.
When she doubts herself, hesitates – I know.
I step up. We are one.
We are Australian.

I came to be because of generosity.
Sheila Woodcock named me,
in honour of her husband.
I am, we are, Australian.

Our Tribe know us as
Guide Dog Woody & The Blind Chick.
We inspire, we encourage,
"have a go, keep trying."
They are no longer… alone.
We are Australian.

I'm a teller of stories, my book is out soon.
I'm not the Police Dog in the street
I'm not the Husky in the snow.
I'm on the farm guiding, using all I know.
I'm the one who waltzed with Matilda.
I am Australian.

I am peace of mind for her family and friends.
They rest easy, my guiding makes amends.
I watch her train her horse.
Her quest to improve
never deviates from the course.
I marvel at how she was born into darkness.
Yet she takes up and holds the reins of life.
I am, we are Australian.

Our sunburnt country dishes up
good times and bad.
I navigate Aussie deadlies,
things that slither and bite.
I endure drought and flooding rains because...
I must!
I am the Sunshine for my Blind Chick.
I am the Spirit of this great land.
I am Australian.

We are one, my Blind Chick and I.
But we help many.
We share a reality –
Vision is much more than Seeing.
I am, We are, Australian.

www.**TheBlindChick**.com.au

*

WELL HELLO

©Guide Dogs NSW

Well, hello!
Firstly, thank you for choosing our book to read. It is a journey about a beautiful horse called Lola, an amazing Guide Dog called Woody, yes that's me, and a beautiful lady called Sue-Ellen, who we lovingly refer to as 'The Blind Chick.'

This is about our journey together: how we met, what we have brought to each other's lives, and how important it is to have friends, independence, and mobility.

It is a wonderful journey. I have a very, very important job to do.

I'm going to be a Guide Dog!

But wait, before I tell you what that means, let me tell you of a big decision we had to make. That of who would go first to introduce themselves: Lola, the Blind Chick or me? Who will it be that starts telling you all about what's involved when a new animal, whether it be a dog or a horse, comes into your life? Especially when such an animal comes into our Blind Chick's life!

The Blind Chick must learn to adapt to how that new horse feels; its size, its temperament, its personality, is it quiet or flighty? The later things are especially difficult for the Blind Chick to interpret though, if it is spooky or jumpy why is that so?

Why? Because she can't see what is upsetting the horse.

So, when she first got Lola, she spent a lot of time getting to know Lola on the ground, and building a relationship. Oh, in case you're not familiar with that term, 'on the ground' means when you're not riding it, when you are training the horse with your two feet on the ground. Another word we might mention is 'lunging.' That's when you have a long rope with one end clipped onto the horse's head collar or bridle, and you stand about 20 metres away from them, holding the other end. They circle around you doing whatever you ask them to do; walk, trot, canter... prance!

The getting to know the new horse on the ground is, when you think about it, it's the extra fun part. You're getting to know somebody new.

And boy oh boy, after getting to know a new horse, imagine what it's been like for the Blind Chick to meet her new Guide Dog!

Yes, okay, she has had six Guide Dogs in the past 38 years, BUT the last two years she hasn't had a Guide Gog. Why? Because she thought she could do without them. But the white cane can only do so much guiding the Blind Chick around, and when it is overcast, she can get lost lot in the garden! Well, to be truthful, she can get lost in her bedroom! But that's another story altogether.

Considering whether it is right to get a new Guide Dog has been a mighty big decision for our Blind Chick.

Give some thought to what it would be like relying on a dog to guide you around? Having the confidence to believe in what the dog is doing, and where the dog is taking you is huge. The time it takes to train one of these amazing dogs, called Guide Dogs, the time it takes for the Blind Chick to trust, to believe in the beautiful Woody, is a truly amazing journey.

There will be lots of laughter I am sure, and sometimes tears, but that's reality, that's life.

So buckle up for the three of us sharing our ups downs with you. The good things, the bad things, the weird things, and the things we don't understand.

It is also an opportunity to explain how very important it is to take one day at a time, and one step at a time, and let things take the time it takes. We'll also share how important kindness and love is. And explore how love makes the world go around and how much difference a smile can make, simply by saying "good morning," or "have a lovely day" - and meaning it!

So once again, we get back to who goes first!

Hmm, maybe it should be the beautiful Lola, because she was the first of us into our Blind Chick's life? But oops no, sorry, it's my book and I'm way to excited to wait any longer. I can't wait to share with you about my life - from a puppy and being trained as a Guide Dog to then coming to live on the farm in Dubbo with the Blind Chick, Sue-Ellen, husband Matthew and their enormous fluffy cat known affectionately as Thunder Paws.

Then our Blind Chick will introduce herself and give you a chance to walk in her shoes.

So, let's get this journey started. Enjoy the ride.

Woody

*

ABOUT ME

Before   After   ©Guide Dogs NSW

I was born to Guide!

Let me first share with you a little bit about myself. While I'm supposed to be a pure-bred Labrador, about two or three generations back I think my great Grandaddy may have been a Golden Retriever. Why? Because I'm quite a leggy Labrador and have quite a fluffy tail. I must say, I do lose a lot of hair. Or so my Blind Chick keeps telling me. It's everywhere!

I am golden in colour and extremely handsome. As you can tell I'm also quite shy. Ha ha!

Like all very special dogs; sheep dogs, cattle dogs, sniffer dogs and truffle dogs, we all have a special job to do. Mine, I was born to lead.

After my first eight weeks with my mum, her name is Shirley, my dad is Raffy, I was taken to the vet. Oh my heavens, I had quite a few needles, but I needed to, they help keep me healthy. Weird was having something squirted up my nose! That was so I don't get kennel cough. One of the needle things didn't have a liquid in it, it had a microchip! That was so if I'm ever lost all someone has to do is run the scanner over the middle of my neck and voila, all my details will come up. Yes, that's certainly a lot to cope with for a young lad but it was pretty cool, I wasn't frightened. Why not? Because my brothers and sisters were with me, all six of us went together.

Yes, in my litter mum had six puppies, all quite cute of course, but definitely not as handsome as me.

We all went to people called Puppy Walkers. I was given to a lovely young lady called Paige, I loved it. She was on a farm and had horses, other dogs and pussycats. It was a pretty cool life.

Apparently, now this is only hearsay mind you, I was a little adventurous and the class clown when I was a young pup. But I wasn't meaning to be naughty, well not deliberately anyway. I have an inquisitive mind, so they soon learnt that to stop me being 'naughty' all they needed to do was keep me busy.

The Puppy Walking was very, very cool. I learnt to go on a lead, to sit, to stop, maybe not chase the pussycat, and to watch Paige while she fed her horses. I was never allowed in with the horses though, they were much bigger than I and while they could have trod on with me, they were very well behaved.

During my puppy walking I also did a couple of TV appearances. Like I said I'm pretty handsome, and that was cool fun. Paige did an interview about puppy walking me and how important donating to Guide Dogs is.

After spending quite a bit of time, I think about a year, with my wonderful puppy walker Paige, I started going to Guide Dog School. Now this was really, really interesting. There were lots of other dogs there, all of us training to become Guide Dogs. What does being a Guide Dog mean? We have to look after blind and visually impaired people. Our job is to guide them safely when they go shopping, to public places, on planes, on trains, on buses, in cars, anywhere and everywhere. Yes wow! How exciting for me, I could end up anywhere.

Did you know the law says we can guide our person anywhere except two places? Can you guess what they are? One is a place where you may have even visited, it has big and small scary and not so scary animals living there. The other has big and small not so scary people living in it, very sick people.

The only places we can't go are zoo's and into a hospital's intensive care units. Both no go zones are to protect those inside from any hygiene or health issues we may have.

Well, Day 1 at Guide Dog School was certainly interesting. The first new thing was getting introduced to what they call a harness. Straight away we started going for walks with this funny harness thing on. It has straps that make it fit snuggly on my body and a handle thing for the human to hold onto with one hand, usually their left hand. For our Blind Chick that works well as she leads the horse with the right hand.

My Guide Dog handler would hold the handle and give me commands. I learnt to walk down the street and stop and sit at the curb, then told forward and I would walk across the street. There were funny lights that beeped a lot in the city, they are called traffic lights. When they're green you can walk across the pedestrian crossing, but when they are red you can't. When they make that particular beep, beep, beep, beep sound, it's telling you – Walk On! This was really cool and really very easy. I was enjoying the training. I would also go out in a van with a few other Guide Dogs. Not all of us will make it as Guide Dogs you know.

Training sure was a lot of fun and I learnt a lot. We went on trains, we went for walks around the street, we walked along the river, I met other dogs in the street which I ignored and walked on guiding my Guide Dog handler like I was asked to do. All in all this Puppy School stuff was a great experience. I learnt so much, but the biggest thing was that I had to look after who I was guiding.

Aagh! Then that Covid thing came along. My training came to a bit of a halt, until... December 2021 when I went for a long drive in a car with Hayley, one of the lovely Guide Dog handlers. We were off to a place in the central west of New South Wales, about five hours drive inland from Sydney, called Dubbo. I was excited about going to a farm because I used to work and live on a farm when I was a puppy.

It was really, really exciting. I was going to be trialled by a blind person to be her Guide Dog.

I remember Hayley mentioning to the blind lady when we got there that when we stopped and turned down the road I stood up. I must've known where I was going. I was just a little excited.

As soon as we arrived to the farm, I was met by Sue-Ellen and her husband Matthew. Wow! It was really nice and green, and Hayley gave Sue-Ellen my lead and we went and sat on a chair in the garden and talked for a while.

This was cool fun, and I got lots of hugs and cuddles. We then went for a walk down the road, but we had someone else come with us. It was Sue-Ellen's horse Lola. Now there's something weird about Sue-Ellen that I need to tell you. Everybody calls her the Blind Chick! So I am going to call her the Blind Chick from now on. Now don't worry, I'm not being rude by calling her that. Why? Because 'The Blind Chick' is the nickname Sue-Ellen gave herself many years ago.

So, Hayley with me on a lead, Matthew leading Lola in one hand and the Blind Chick in the other, we all went for a walk down the driveway. We walked out about not quite half a kilometre, then returned to walk back, and the Blind Chick said to Hayley; "is it okay if we put the harness on and Woody guides me home?" Well guess what! I was super excited! This was my first real walk with a blind person. Woohoo, bring it on!

So, the harness is put on me and its now my job to lead the Blind Chick back home. So we stand quietly, the Blind Chick says " up Woody," and I walk off leading with great confidence. It was so cool. So we walked back down the road and into the garden and then Hayley quickly popped through in front of us and the Blind Chick said to me, "follow Woody, follow." I followed Hayley back to the garden seat. Wow wow and wow! We did our first official Guide Dog walk. Woohoo, this was totally awesome!

And I didn't mind walking with Lola either. She just stayed with Matthew, and I walked along with Hayley, and they talked on the way back. I admit it, I did a great job guiding the Blind Chick.

We also did a couple of other things; I followed Matthew up to the place called the Dressage arena. This is where the Blind Chick rides her horse Lola. So we did a few little walks out there doing destination work. What does 'destination work' mean I hear you ask? The 'destination' is the place I need to go, the Blind Chick just has to say that word, like: arena, tack shed, round yard... She often prefaces it with 'Find', for example "Find Arena", "Find Tack Shed".

When I got to the mounting block, which the Blind Chick stands on to get on Lola, I was given a treat. Boy I do love treats!

So this was turning out pretty darn cool. I then walked the Blind Chick back to the garden and to the chair we were sitting on. I did this all by myself, no help from Hayley this time, I'm clever (and modest!)

But farm life wasn't to last! I was put back in the car and we drove away. I didn't get to stay with the Blind Chick. I went back to Sydney with Hayley, where I was taken back to a homestay place for Guide Dogs. But nothing happened for ages.

Then there was movement at the station. I had started going out on walks again with the Guide Dog trainer, until... I was given a new trainer, a lady called Danni. Maybe, just maybe we might be going back to visit the Blind Chick. Maybe, just maybe, I might get to stay.

So, keep reading to see what happens next. To see what adventures we go on. I hope you enjoy my journey. I am having a blast!

Your friend

Woody

Guide Dog Extraordinaire

Putting my best foot forward
©MegRose Photography

*

Tribute to my Blind Chick

For Sue my Hero

by Bob Cooper

She lives in constant shadows, the darkness of the night,
But strength is her companion in the ever-fading light,
Sue may be blind to others, she is not blind to me,

For I have found her secret, that my friend Sue can see.
Though eyesight may elude her, I have known it from the start,
She doesn't need the eyesight, for Sue sees with her heart.

Her sense of hearing , smell, and touch,
are sharpened by her plight,
Her kind deeds and compassion have kept her from the night.
And no complaints are offered, affliction is her shield,
A knight in shining armour, upon life's battlefield.

We loose our way, we rarely hear the song bird in the tree,
And often we blunder through life with things we will not see.

Her great love for her animals , her courage through each trial,
Her great determination, still leaves me with a smile,

I know that others call her blind, it matters not to me,
For I have found her secret, that my friend Sue can see.

*

LET ME INTRODUCE YOU TO MY BLIND CHICK

"Let me be your eyes"   ©MegRose Photography

I'd like to start early in our story by introducing you to someone who is the centre of my universe! They are the most important character in my life, my Blind Chick. Well, that's what I call her. Her real name is Sue-Ellen Lovett.

Nothing happens in the Blind Chick's world without help from her wonderful friends and family.

She is one very cool lady and I have just jotted down a few things below that you might like to know about her. Oh my, she is quite a high achiever. Did you know I am her seventh Guide Dog? Lucky me. She'll be able to continue my training.

But before we go on, I need to let you know of a little typo in this chapter. Yes, it's true the Blind Chick's first Guide Dog was called Eccles, but hmm, he's described as being her best Guide Dog ever! Well, I'm sure she has reassessed that situation now, hee hee. By a country mile I am the most charismatic, handsome, loyal and wonderful Guide Dog. I guide and look after my Blind Chick every day. Maybe it's around the farm and on our trips. We make an awesome team.

I hope you enjoy learning about my Blind Chick. I'm very proud of her. She's not big on singing her own praises, so I've had to listen into other people's conversations when they speak about all the amazing awards she's received and all the incredible things she's done.

I suspect even after a lifetime with her I'll still not have compiled the full list of things that show what a generous kind person she is, and a brilliant teacher! I can certainly vouch for that. Just seeing how well I do my job is a reflection of my Blind Chick's mastery. She's incredibly humble but I get why. She doesn't do all the life changing stuff she does to get the praise, she does it because it's in her DNA, it's how she's wired. It's who she is. Lucky me to walk beside her every day, well actually not quite beside her, I'm always a little in front, hee hee, guiding her.

Here goes the list I've compiled so far. Stay tuned for additions as I learn them.

Dual Paralympian, Atlanta 1996 & Sydney 2000, Bronze Medallist at the 1999 World Dressage Championships in Denmark where she was ranked 4th in the World, Ranked in the Top 10% of Elite Dressage Riders in Australia, Cancer Survivor, Fundraiser of $3.2 million for various charities by doing 10 marathon long distance endurance rides on horseback, Director on the Paralympic Games Committee Board, Author, Wife and Horse Addict.

My Blind Chick was born in Mudgee and now lives with husband Matthew on a farm in Dubbo. She has had six Guide Dogs in the past 38 years and was always accompanied by one of her Guide Dogs, even when competing internationally at World Championships and Paralympics. Yes, her Guide Dogs accumulated a serious amount of Frequent Flyer Points!

Her most famous Guide Dog (until now!) was Eccles, a creamy lab with golden spots on his ears who accompanied her to Denmark, Atlanta, and Sydney. My Blind Chick endearingly refers to him as her Suit and Tie dog, because he was always so professional.

Now there's something important for you to know. My Blind Chick isn't a little bit blind, she is TOTALLY blind. By this I mean she doesn't see any shades of grey, her world is all black. But as you can tell by this incomplete summary of her achievements, a list that'd make even the most ardent award collector gag, she continues to overcome the limitations that come with not being able to see anything with her eyes. But boy oh boy does she have vision of the more important kind. What she sees with her heart and mind continues to shock and surprise me. I'm not sure if I'll ever get used to Guiding someone who has more 'vision' than a sighted person!

How did she become blind you ask? She was born with a hereditary disease called Retinitis Pigmentosa. But she didn't know as a child that what she could see, which was only about 12 percent, wasn't normal. Hence she was known as a bit of a 'clumsy child', until she was 12 and got diagnosed. It was in her thirties that the decline of her sight stopped declining. Why? Because it couldn't get any less.

But my Blind Chick is amazing. She doesn't let her lack of sight stop her achieving her goals, on or off the saddle. She 'Lives to Ride', she competes at FEI Inter 1 level, and trains Grand Prix.

As well as riding, her life is devoted to helping and motivating people. During the long-distance marathon endurance rides she raised $3.2 million dollars for various charities. Along those rides she'd speak at the various events giving inspirational talks to hundreds and thousands of people. All up she spoke at over 600 towns and cities. Can you imagine that!

Her biggest gig was to an audience of over 50,000 people, while on the back of Mudgee, her beloved stock horse mare, at the MCG in Melbourne. I wish I'd been there. That would have been incredible. I wish I could meet Mudgee but sadly that's not possible. Mudgee died a few years ago. But I know by the stories my Blind Chick tells me about her that while Mudgee may be gone, she is certainly not forgotten.

One of my Blind Chick's longest fundraising rides was from Cairns to the Gold Coast. Yes, that's a seriously long way, 2400 km, 54 days in the saddle, with the funds raised going to the RDA. Another was from Melbourne to Sydney to raise money and public awareness for the Sydney 2000 Paralympic Games. At that time she was short listed to be competing in the Australian Team at the Sydney Paralympics, yet even with all the training for that, she still did the 38 days in the saddle and raised $1.1m.

Did you know she's also an author? In 2020 her heart-warming story about love, achievement, overcoming adversity and daring to dream through the big brown eyes of her horse Johno was published. Johno & The Blind Chick gives readers a unique insight into the remarkable journey of this beautiful horse and his once-in-a-lifetime rider, from the moment they first met.

Then in 2021 Johno & The Blind Chick 2 was released. Then in 2023 the Blind Chick's autobiography, so named, was launched. In 2024 will be the release of a documentary about her life, in which I feature as a star character of course.

Life with my Blind Chick is certainly never dull.

And wow! As I write this, we've only been together seven months.

And there's more!

It was only when I started looking at all Sue-Ellen's achievements that I got to realise the generosity and magnitude of her 40+ years spent helping others.

This amazing woman is to humble to include such a list in this book. But I couldn't wait to share with you a snapshot of highlights of her life... so far.

Yes, she's not done yet!

Perhaps you'll be lucky enough to join her on her next adventure?

Australian of Year Nomination 1991: Paul Keating, John Newcomb &
Sue-Ellen. Sue-Ellen receiving the Australian Achievers Medal

Degree of Difficulty of the Achievement and Sacrifices Made
Sue-Ellen is TOTALLY blind. She doesn't even have shades of
black.

- EVERY day Sue-Ellen gets lost trying to navigate around
  her own back yard
- EVERY day Sue-Ellen gets zapped by one of the properties
  electric fences
- EVERY day Sue-Ellen walks into something ouch; a wall, a
  tree, a table, a bucket, a snake!
- EVERY day this lady gets out of bed, gives generously to
  others and changes peoples and companies lives and
  financial positions with her determination and commitment
  to Make A Difference and Be A Positive Role Model.

Funds Raised
$3.2 million for various charities raised by doing 10 long-distance
horse rides.

Years of Service
40 years of FREE Service. None of Sue-Ellen's four decades of
service in Australia have ever been paid for.

Reach

950+	**number of speaking engagements** delivered (fundraising, inspiration, life lessons, showing ability not disability, overcoming adversity, If its going to be – its up to me.
50,000+	**number of people reached via speaking engagements** * Largest speaking gig was at the Melbourne Cricket Ground to a packed crowd, 22,000 in attendance. She was riding her best horse mate Mudgee while presenting!
650+	**number of towns/cities/hamlets** presented to
Thousands	**International and National audience** – Johno & The Blind Chick Facebook Influencer

Magic Moments

- The only totally blind equestrian to ride at Grand Prix level - in the world.
- Representing Australia in the Paralympics – Atlanta (1996) & Sydney (2000)
- Represented Australia at the World Equestrian Games in Denmark (1999) – Bronze Medallist
- Ranked 4th in the world in Dressage at the World Equestrian Games
- Ranked in the Top 10% of Elite Dressage Riders in Australia
- Australian of the Year Finalist (1991)
- Won Young Citizen of the Year Award – Mudgee, twice
- Australian Sport Medal – endorsed by the Queen
- Author of 3 books (2020, 2021, 2022), being sold internationally, 4th in the pipeline
- Competed solely in able bodied competitions since 2000.
- Wife of 20+ years
- Cancer Survivor
- Documentary on her life – due out in 2023

*

QUESTIONS MOST PEOPLE AREN'T GAME TO ASK! PT 1

"Happiness is a Choice"
Sue-Ellen Lovett

Walking with my two mates   ©MegRose Photography

It's interesting! I've been doing speaking gigs for years and people always have questions but there are many questions people aren't game to ask. So, I thought I'd shed some light on some of those questions you are too afraid to ask or that I've heard murmured in corridors and behind my back.

I hope by sharing these answers with you it helps put a lid on many misconceptions and inaccurate assumptions.

WHY ARE YOU CALLED THE BLIND CHICK?

Don't be shocked by the answer – guess who gave me 'The Blind Chick' nickname?

A name that has stuck for over 40 years! I gave it to myself! Yes.

I remember as a wee child being called the Blind Chickie Babe. Some people may find being called 'Blind' offensive, like a person in a wheelchair being called a 'Wheelie', but let's not get so politically correct we're blind to the truth.

Like it or not, I am blind.

Hence, I'm not offended if you call me The Blind Chick. It's who I am and... I'm proud of who I am.

DO YOU KNOW WHAT YOUR HUSBAND MATTHEW LOOKS LIKE?

A Day to Remember – 22 April 2000   ©Debra Lovett

No!

But we fall in love with what's inside someone, not what they look like.

I met my lovely husband Matthew through my coach Judy Cubitt. I'd gone to Dubbo to train in preparation for hopefully qualifying for the Sydney Paralympic games. We stayed at Matthew's Mum and Dad's property and Matthew was there. I'll touch on what happened next in the book.

What is one of your most embarrassing moments?

Wow this one is an easy one. I was not just embarrassed, I was mortified.

It was amongst people that I knew. I was doing a speaking engagement for Riding For The Disabled Mudgee New South Wales in my hometown of Mudgee. I was up on stage presenting, I'd been on stage for probably half an hour when I heard a lone giggle, then more giggles!

Then out of the blue a long time friend of mine, Huey Bateman, said to somebody "would someone please go and turn her around so she is facing the crowd, this is really bad and embarrassing for all."

Someone quietly came up to the stage and touched my arm and turned me to face the crowd then explained to me how I'd been standing with my side to the audience that whole time, talking to a wall! I was horrified, I was embarrassed. I don't think I'd ever felt so gutted in my entire life, that someone would let me stand and speak to a wall. Oh my lord, I'd never been so humiliated. But as you do, I made out there was a funny side to it and got on with finishing my presentation. But it wasn't funny, it was humiliating. I had a major meltdown afterwards at the magnitude of the embarrassment. Now every time I do a presentation I hold onto a lectern, and I make sure I'm facing the crowd. I don't ever want to experience that level of embarrassment again.

Aren't you terrified when you ride a horse, and you can't see?

NO – people forget what it's like to be a kid. I'm still connected to that inner child. (I still love my pony.)

Five year old me on Sugar in the days when helmets weren't a thing.

COULD YOU IMAGINE YOUR LIFE WITHOUT A HORSE?

That is a definite no! I could never imagine my life without a horse. I could never imagine my life without animals in it. They bring pure magic and love to my life. The horse has two beautiful brown eyes that make up for my eyes that don't see (by the way, my eyes are hazel.)

So definitely, I could not imagine my life without my beautiful horse. The joy I get just going down and feeding my horse, brushing her, spending time with her, going for a walk. It's a simple thing, life for me without a horse is not a life. They bring pure magic to my life, every day. They make my dreams come true. They make it all worthwhile.

HOW MANY GUIDE DOGS HAVE YOU HAD AND WHY DO YOU RETIRE THEM?

Well sometimes you don't have a choice about when you retire your Guide Dog.

My first beautiful Guide Dog was Donna, she was a German Shepherd who died from pancreatic cancer. The rest of my Guide Dogs retired because they got to a stage where they were possibly incontinent, getting a little bit slow and/or a little bit arthritic. You generally get seven maybe eight years, if you're really lucky nine years out of a Guide Dog. My last Guide Dog Armani I retired early because I thought I didn't need a Guide Dog anymore. I wasn't using her at home and I was worried about her being bitten by a snake. But after the last two years without one, I've realised I definitely need a Guide Dog. Bring it on!

IS YOUR GUIDE DOG ALSO YOUR PET?

No. Absolutely not!

My Guide Dog is my work tool. I give them praise for doing the right thing, I don't have it sitting on my lap or shower it with love to bits, they are very very much a Guide Dog. They have a job to do and to support them doing their job I am very strict about people not interfering with my Guide Dog. Please don't pat the Guide Dog, please don't feed the dog, otherwise the Blind Chick bites, ha ha.

WHY DO YOU WEAR DARK GLASSES IF YOU CAN'T SEE?

Often when I am doing a presentation, I wear my dark glasses. Sometimes I take them off halfway through, to prove a point.

I think perhaps I hide behind the glasses sometimes. Why? Because my eyes look normal! My retina is the thing that's died, that makes me not see, so if people see my eyes oh my heavens, the first thing they say is "oh she can see! She can see more than she says." I found it very hard in the early stages of going blind to cope with this.

I also wear dark glasses when I'm outside to stop the pain. My left eye is totally black but my right eye is totally white with fog. So if the sun gets on my right eye the pain I get from the glare is enormous, it makes me nauseous ... it's that bad. Hence the dark glasses outside.

DO YOU EVER FEEL LIKE YOU'RE INCONVENIENCING PEOPLE?

Absolutely! On a daily basis.

There are so many things I can't do. Like something as simple as knowing what's inside a can that I've taken from the pantry; is it cat food, is it dog food, is it pumpkin soup or chicken soup. It's the little things that have to be done on a daily basis like "can you please tell me how many calories are in this" that might annoy people (a lot!). When you live this constant enquiry about simple things day in, day out, I'm sure it gets wearing. But I try to be as independent as I can.

I now have some apps on my phone that read labels to me, so I'm a little more independent.

IS IT HARD ASKING FOR HELP?

I can ask for help for someone else, every hour of the day, if that asking makes a difference to their life, but I truly struggle asking for help myself.

Yes, I feel compromised. It is a really hard one for me to get my head around. I try to be as independent and capable as I can, but sometimes you really do have to be brave and just ask for help.

DO YOU EVER FEEL USED?

Wow, wow and wow! This is a confronting question.

Yes, I find it hard to ask for help.

Having the NDIS has made the world of difference because I can now afford to pay someone to help me. Previously I would often find myself in a situation where I was unable to do things for myself and while people would offer to help, they'd done so because it was cool or a novelty to help the blind girl, "I'm doing something for the blind girl," "I'm taking the blind girl here."

That often made me feel funny in the tummy, but someone helping you is still someone helping you and I was very grateful. Hence, I've often felt like I was the novelty friend. And invariably, that novelty soon wears off.

*

BORD TO LEAD

"Don't always follow the herd, you can be the Leader".
©MegRose Photography

MY JOB DESCRIPTION

You may know of me as a Guide Dog, but I've got another name for what I do. I'm also called a Service dog. I've been breed for the job of assisting people who are blind or partially sighted. I was born to lead.

I'm a Labrador and the most common of the preferred breed for Guide Dogs in Australia. The other breed used is the Golden Retriever. How's this for a fun fact - I've got the best of both breeds in my DNA! Yes, my great grand daddy was a Golden Retriever. I can thank him for my extra long legs, my fluffy tail and my extra handsomeness.

While our breed may vary, what doesn't is that we must embody the characteristics that are essential to good guiding.

Ok, let's talk essential characteristics.

First there's our **TEMPRAMENT**.

Blind people must navigate with their Guide Dogs through any number of places, some of which may be crowded, such as shopping centres, city streets, subway terminals and airports. Dogs trained to be Guide Dogs, therefore, must be ready to tackle situations that might be overwhelming for other dogs. Guide Dogs must remain focused on their task, and not become easily distracted by loud noises or unfamiliar smells and sights. They must be calm and friendly. Guide Dogs must never react aggressively, even if people step on them accidentally or pet them without permission.

Next is that we must have above average **BRAINS**, **INTELLIGENCE** and **TRAINABILITY**. And boy oh boy have I got oodles of all those traits!

Dogs trained to be Guide Dogs must be intelligent. Guide Dogs must help their owners get through any number of obstacles unscathed. They must also understand and obey commands. The owner must always be in control. However, Guide Dogs must be intelligent enough to know when to disobey a command that puts the owner in danger. For example, if a dog is asked to cross the street while cars are coming, he must know to disobey.

My **BRAINS**, **INTELLIGENCE**, **TRAINABILITY** and **CONFIDENCE** make me the perfect Guide Dog. Why? Because those are the critical things that mean I can keep my person safe, I'll make the decisions they don't have the eyes to make. Without **TRUST**, we have nothing.

Creating a **PERFECT MATCH**!

Before I got to meet my Blind Chick, the people at Guide Dogs NSW spent a serious amount of time going through the list of things that ensure we would be a good match. The list includes; Environment, personality, temperament, body sizes and experience. My Blind Chick and I are a perfect match because we both have similar temperaments and personalities, both of us are quite outgoing. We walk with confidence together whenever we're working, we move as one, smoothly, easily. Nothing is a drama when we're together. And bonus! We both love the outdoors.

Practically what does this mean? Let's look at how they matched **BODY SIZES**. Guide Dogs must be large enough to lead their owners while wearing a harness. They should not be so large that the owner cannot control the Guide Dog easily. Because Guide Dogs are always with their owners in any type of situation, they should ideally fit comfortable on public transportation, such as subways and buses, and beneath tables in restaurants. They need to fit in the foot well of a car, albeit I can do this but not for long because I'm quite tall, it can get uncomfortable.

HEALTH AND STAMINA

The **PHYSICAL**! I passed my physical with flying colors. I'm healthy and have lots of stamina. Understandably the health of a Guide Dog is critical. I've been told we cost a lot to train, so to make that investment worthwhile we need to work for many years. Before we start our training, our health is fully screened. Dogs who are genetically prone to illness don't get trained. As soon as a Guide Dog starts to show any illness or abnormalities, such as hip dysplasia, they are retired from service work.

Welcome to my world.

Your friend

Woody

Guide Dog Extraordinaire

*

GUIDE DOG ETIQUETTE

Please don't…

CAN I PAT YOUR GUIDE DOG WHILE IT IS IN HARNESS?

This is an, absolutely NO!
Please do not pat mine or any Guide Dog in a harness. Please don't make eye contact with them. They'll take that as you engaging with them. Wearing their harness is how the Guide Dog knows they are working. It's really important when they are guiding me or even just sitting beside me relaxing, and they are in harness, that they not to be disturbed or distracted.

Keep in mind they are responsible for my life! I don't want my Guide Dog seeing you in another 20 minutes and thinking, "oh there's that nice person who patted me" and get distracted and not let me know there are steps in front of me and I fall down them.

It is critical Guide Dogs doesn't get distracted while working.

MAY I FEED YOUR GUIDE DOG WHILE IT IS IN HARNESS?

This also is an absolutely NO!
For the previous reason, but I will reiterate that while the Guide Dog's harness is on it, they must not get distracted by someone patting them , feeding them, whistling, or calling out to them. They have a very, very responsible job. They are looking after my life.

DO YOU EVER TAKE YOUR GUIDE DOG OUT OF HARNESS SO SOMEONE CAN PAT IT?

As a rule, not unless the Guide Dog is off work and then I 'may' allow them to interact and have a pat.

But I don't encourage it.

I really would like one hundred percent of my Guide Dog's attention and commitment to stay focused. They all have playtime. Woody will play and fetch the ball for Matthew, and Matthew toilets him. But Woody's focus is always on me, and I would like it to stay that way.

Understandably I don't overly encourage people's interaction with my Guide Dog. Maybe when we get a little further down the track and our relationship is a little more solid and established, I may allow this to happen on the very odd occasion, but it is not something I encourage or do very often.

DO YOU ENCOURAGE OTHER GUIDE DOGS TO INTERACT WITH YOUR GUIDE DOG WHILE THEY ARE WORKING?

Absolutely NOT!

This again is another distraction. It is really lovely when you go walking and people have their dogs on the lead and not running free. I have had the misfortune with one of my Guide Dogs being attacked by dogs off lead. This is a very scary situation for me and my Guide Dog, plus extremely dangerous.

DO YOU ALLOW YOUR GUIDE DOG TO PLAY WITH OTHER DOGS WHEN THEY ARE OUT OF HARNESS?

Personally, I don't.

My mother and father-in-law who live in the property next to Matt and I, have a lovely little caboodle called Bonnie. She will come over and visit on the odd occasion, but we don't encourage this at all. When I take Woody out to play sometimes Bonnie comes and sits and watches. But he is so big, and he could roll her over very quickly as she is an older girl. So, it is important to be considerate of other dogs when you have a big dog like Woody.

IS DOG DISTRACTION A PROBLEM IN TOWN?

Sometimes, depending on the Guide Dogs distraction issues. This can be an issue with dogs tied on the back of Utes growling and barking as you go past. This can sometimes strike a nerve with your Guide Dog. But then there are other Guide Dogs that pay absolutely no attention to the yapping, barking dog, and you just say 'Leave It, Walk On', and everything is fine.

So this really does depend on each individual Guide Dog.

CAN FOOD DROPPED ON THE GROUND BE A DISTRACTION TO YOUR GUIDE DOG WORKING?

Once again this is an issue with individual Guide Dogs.

Some of them have terrible food distraction, while others will walk past and ignore it.

I think the best thing if you realise the dog is trying to get at some of the food, you can distract them back to you by saying 'Leave It, Walk On' or by offering a treat reward yourself for walking past and ignoring. The food distraction can be handled in many ways, but I would prefer my Guide Dog to ignore it. Which is what Woody normally does.

WHERE DOES YOUR GUIDE DOG SIT WHEN YOU'RE TRAVELLING IN A CAR FROM POINT A TO POINT B?

With all my other Guide Dogs they have all sat at my feet in the front foot well. This can't happen with Woody though, as he is such a large dog. He goes in the back section of our SUV on some padding and his spare dog bed. He's very comfortable. He is tied in the back so he's not loose in case of an accident or he gets distracted. Safety first.

DO YOU USE WOODY OUT OF HARNESS?

Woody is an exceptional Guide Dog.
From about day five we have been going out and toileting with him not in harness. Which is extremely fast learning to do a behaviour where he doesn't have his harness on.

He stops at the top of the steps and guides me down one at a time, he then walks out along the path, turns right through the Pine Trees, then left down the dirt road, I walk about seven steps, I ask him to sit, and then I say to him "quick, quick, Woody, quick, quick." And he goes and toilets himself off lead.

This is exceptional for a Guide Dog to be doing this in such a short time, and he does it with such ease. Then once he has finished his business, he comes back to me, sits by my side, and I say, "inside Woody, inside." He goes about eight steps back, turns right, then turns left, up the path, stops at the steps, I give him the okay, we go up the steps one at a time, then he goes and sits on his bed.

He truly is an exceptional Guide Dog. Lucky me.

DO YOU ALLOW WOODY TO WALK AROUND YOUR HORSE WHILE SHE IS TIED UP?

Absolutely NOT!

Dogs and horses aren't a very good combination at the best of times. Doing that would be a quick way to get Woody kicked or for your horse to tread on your dog. I only use Woody in harness around my horse and when we are at the tack shed and Woody is not leading Lola and I, he is tethered to a drum next to the tack shed, to keep him safe.

I always keep a healthy distance between him and Lola while I am saddling up. This is for safety's sake. Keep in mind, I am totally blind, and I would hate for my beautiful Woody to be hurt or for Lola to get a fright because Woody moved quickly or did something to startle the situation.

I always try to keep things safe, to minimise the risk of injury.

DO YOU TAKE WOODY WITH YOU WHEN YOU GO AWAY TRAINING WITH YOUR HORSE?

Absolutely!

We will be doing lots of going away and training, Woody will always be with us because he is responsible for guiding Lola and I to the destinations like a dressage arena, once he is orientated and knows where he is going, and what he is doing.

Being such a quick learner, this won't take long. I am looking forward to our first trip away in a few weeks in fact.

IS DISCIPLINE IMPORTANT WITH A GUIDE DOG?

Absolutely! Discipline, consistency, kindness, and a lot of encouragement are the keys to his success.

If you aren't consistent with your training with your Guide Dog in harness, there are going to be issues.

So, the importance of being consistent is paramount.

DO YOU DO OBEDIENCE WORK WITH WOODY OUT OF HARNESS?

Yes.

I try to do a little bit of obedience work every day. I integrate it with our playtime in the dressage arena or out in the front yard. Woody loves it. He is now learning to come. I put my hand up and say "stop", and he stays. Then I call him.

I think this is an important command in case something goes very wrong. Safety is a big thing. I love obedience work and I love an obedient dog.

DO YOU TELL YOUR GUIDE DOG A COMMAND MANY TIMES?

No, generally it is one command.

Sit, or stay, or forward, or down, left, or right. Unless it is when my Guide Dog isn't listening. Woody is exceptional with all his commands.

I think if I was a Guide Dog, or any animal, or even a child, I'd hate having the same word said over and over. I'd hate being nagged at. So, if I teach him something, for those first times we do it he gets lots of praise, maybe even a treat! But nagging is definitely out.

WHAT IS YOUR PET DISLIKE WHEN OUT WITH YOUR GUIDE DOG?

This is easy to answer.

It's someone trying to distract my Guide Dog from the very important job of looking after me.

*

My new family

One for All, All for One
@2C Photography @Guide Dogs NSW

Being part of the family!
What does 'family' look like for me? I'm an integral part as our Blind Chick's life. I give her more independence and mobility and increase the choices she has for what she does with her life, and what she can do with her horses.

Lucky for me my 'family' here in Dubbo means I get to be a farm boy! There are so many extra things I get to do and the extra freedoms I have. It's pretty amazing and so much fun.

How many Guide Dogs get to go running beside their blind person who is on a motorbike or on the tandem pushbike while they go out fencing or checking the crops. Being part of this family is pretty cool.

Apart from me bringing so many amazing things to the Blind Chick's life, she has enriched my life. Plus I now have a new mate, a very cute fluffy cat called Thunder Paws. And while he took a little bit of winning over, we're now pretty good buddies. Plus there's Lola, the beautiful black horse. She and I have been mates really from day one.

And then there's Matthew! He is the Blind Chick's amazing husband who is just such cool fun. He and I do lots of playing out in the yard together, and sometimes if the Blind Chick is out and about, he'll feed and toilet me. He also toilets me late at night, about 10 o'clock, if the Blind Chick has already gone to bed. This is pretty good of him as a late night wander outside is probably not the best job for our Blind Chick to do

I think, no I know, Matthew considers me the coolest thing since sliced bread, and that I'm the most intelligent of the Blind Chicks previous six Guide Dogs, including the Suit and Tie professional Eccles.

I'm her lucky seventh Guide Dog and I must say I love learning new destinations, doing new things and going exploring on the farm. But it's also pretty cool just sitting with my family on the veranda enjoying a sunset. Life doesn't get much better than that.

And how about how we start each morning. Our routine is that the Blind Chick feeds two kookaburras! Yes, they come and sit on the veranda, laugh and talk to each other while she feeds them.

Yes, life on the farm is interesting. It's certainly never dull. Being part of my family is magical.

Your friend

Woody

Guide Dog Extraordinaire

*

LOLA

Hello there, my name is Lola.
I am 15 years young, a black Warmblood, standing 16.1 hands high, and everyone says I'm beautiful! While I'm not sure about that, I do get lots of compliments. My coat is very shiny, and I love people and carrots.

I was bred down in the Hunter Valley in New South Wales, Australia, by a wonderful lady by the name of Jacinta Ledlan. For many years I lived on her property at Sandy Hollow. It's a beautiful property called Araluen Park. Jacinta has bred many gorgeous horses and is still breeding beautiful horses with her stallions.

I spent a lot of my younger years being a show hack. We went to many places, travelling all around the countryside, like going to the Sydney Royal Easter Show and lots of city and country shows. I also went to the Grand National with a beautiful young girl called

Sara, and we won! How exciting is that! I have also competed in Arab Derivative classes because there is a little bit of Arab back in my breeding profile. This is what gives me my unique classical, beautiful looks.

Through the years I've been very fortunate to be trained in many disciplines. Apart from doing hacking, I also did show jumping and going cross country in the sport called Eventing. I have enjoyed all of it. Jacinta and I used to have loads of fun eventing. Plus we did a bit of dressage. The latter being our Blind Chicks favourite equestrian sport.

My pet hate with any of it, in the training, would be if I was made to do lots and lots of circles, the lunging thing. That's one thing riders seem to do, lots and lots of circles. While it's not my favourite thing, I suppose it must achieve things when you are training.

During my show career I spent lots of time being pampered in beautiful stables. I was brushed – a lot! I lived in the stables with the overhead lights left on until 10 o'clock at night. Why the lights you ask? Show people believe this is to trick my body into thinking its still a warm season so I don't have to grow a thick woolly winter coat. The idea behind the lights being left on is to help keep my coat nice , short and shiny for the show season.

It was always very exciting going to shows. I got to catch up with lots of my mates and go out and do what I do best, be a showgirl and strut my stuff.

At one of these shows though there was a wee accident. I got kicked in the tummy by another horse. This caused a terrible thing called colic. Colic can sometimes be fixed with medication from the vet, but my colic got very bad, as my bowel was twisted. I had to have a very big operation and was touch and go there for a while.

If it wasn't for the love of the beautiful Sara and her mum looking after me, I'm sure I wouldn't have had such a good recovery. Whoohoo me, six months after that surgery I was back in the show ring!

But everybody is now very careful as far as my dietary needs go, to help minimise the risk of me getting colic again. Next time I colic I might not be so lucky!

I had been sitting in the paddock for probably about six months at the beautiful Jacinta's, not doing much at all. Yes I was brought in on the odd occasion to go and do a little bit of cattle work, or for Jacinta to have a play around with me over the show jumps. But other than that, I wasn't doing much at all except be a horse in the paddock.

Oh, I nearly forgot, I also went and had lessons with Robyn Smith. That was really cool as she has a beautiful indoor arena and Jacinta, and I had a few lessons with her. This was good fun.

Unbeknownst to me, Jacinta had read an advertisement about a blind girl looking to buy a horse because the lovely horse she had, called Johno, had to be euthanised because he had a degenerative neurological condition called Equine Shivers. Johno had gotten very sick and quite dangerous. This is the reason why the blind girl was looking for a new horse.

Many days went past and then one special Saturday rolled around. These people in a white ute pulled up. There was a very tall guy who held a girls hand a lot, and then there was another lovely lady who I found out was the tall guy's mum, her name was Lee. The guy's name was Matthew, and he was married to the Blind Chick, her name is Sue-Ellen.

I heard Jacinta telling the Blind Chick, Matthew, and Lee all about me. I was in the yard just standing, hanging around, waiting to see what was going to happen. Jacinta had worked me earlier that morning, and I was still quite sweaty as I had a very woolly winter coat.

Now, I must tell you, I have no idea about this blindness thing, or what it means. But I did notice that apart from Matthew holding the girls hands a lot, guiding her, and telling her where things were, so was her mother-in-law Lee. They were very careful about where she went and what she did, so she knew all the time where she was. And okay, she was at an unfamiliar place, but everyone giving her all these directions, it was like, what is going on here? Slowly but surely, it dawned on me! When you can't see you have to rely on people telling you what is around you, and you do a lot of feeling things.

This became very apparent to me over the next 15 to 20 minutes while the Blind Chick was in the yard with me. She felt my eyes, my ears, my nose, my neck. She felt down my legs, she felt my tummy, where I have a very big scar, she felt all along my back and down my rump. She commented on how woolly I was and that I felt really nice. She did a lot of smiling. I knew straight away that she liked me.

Jacinta helped the Blind Chick saddle me up, and then we went for a walk. Once again, the tall guy Matthew took the Blind Chick's hand and guided her, and we all walked down to the paddock where Jacinta normally trains me. Jacinta asked the Blind Chick whether she wanted to ride first, but she said no if Jacinta would ride first so she could see how I went. Well, there wasn't much seeing was there! She would listen and her wonderful mother-in-law Lee and husband Matthew would describe what was happening.

I must say, I was on my best behaviour. I did some lovely work for Jacinta, just simple stuff; walk, trot and canter in circles and changes of directions. Then it was the Blind Chick's turn. She confidently stood up on the mounting block, they lined me up so she could put her foot in the stirrup and then she mounted. The tall guy Matthew kept talking to her and telling her where to go and to follow him and then we started circling around Matthew. At first, I think the Blind Chick was quite tentative and not quite sure. But as we went on, she relaxed, and she seemed to be enjoying the ride.

Wow! When you think of it, how much trust is she putting in me and her husband Matthew guiding her riding a horse she doesn't know. I will try to be on my best behaviour because I don't want to give her a fright.

While she was riding, she was talking to her husband Matthew. He was giving her feedback on how we looked. She said I was much more forward than any other horse she had ridden. This probably overwhelmed her a little bit in the beginning. But she thought she could get used to my paces; it would just take time.

So, on a lovely big circle we walked, then we trotted, and we cantered. While she was talking, she was relaxing more and more, and not paying too much attention to what was happening. This was a good thing because I think sometimes you can worry about something that isn't going to happen at all. So, with Matthew speaking to her and the conversation between them, she very quickly relaxed, and we had a lovely ride. But I've gotta tell you, this Blind Chick smiles... a lot!

After a few more circling Matthew we moseyed back over to Lee and Jacinta. The Blind Chick was just about to get off and Jacinta said, "would you like to ride her back up to the house?" Well dah! The Blind Chick jumped at this and said, "yes please!" So, the Blind Chick and I walked beside Matthew back up to the house.

I think the Blind Chick thought this was pretty cool. She dismounted, gave me a lovely big pat and revealed something I love from her pocket. Yay, I love carrots! While I chomped on the carrot she told me I was a good girl.

Like a pit crew working together they unsaddled me. Then I was bathed with soap and water, well shampoo and conditioner. I felt really good after my bath as the water got rid of all the sweat.

Matthew held me while Jacinta bathed me, and the Blind Chick and Lee sat and talked about the ride and what she thought of riding me. I wondered if she was going to take me home? Why? Because I'd noticed they had a horse float with them when they arrived. You don't bring a horse float just for the trip, do you?

Next thing I see Jacinta giving the Blind Chick a bridle and saddle and a whole heap of rugs. Oh wow! Looks like I'm going for a sleepover! All of these things were put into the horse float and then the next thing I was on the horse float and doing a road trip. I wonder where I'm going.

To be honest I wasn't sure if I really wanted to leave Jacinta. We have been together for many, many years and I knew I was very special to her because she had named me, my registered name, is 'We Love Lola.' Everyone that meets me seems to love me, a lot, which is very cool.

Well, there were lots of tears, lots of hugs, and promises that they would look after me. Jacinta was happy, but sad seeing me leave. But I think the Blind Chick will look after me really, really well.

Yum, there was a lovely biscuit of lucerne hay in the horse float, lucerne from their farm in Dubbo, so I ate for a couple of hours and then... wow we were somewhere new!

Gee-whiz it's flat out here. Where I came from in the Hunter Valley there are hills and beautiful cliffs and amazing valleys. This was such a contrasting landscape, still gorgeous but very flat and oh heavens, there's a river! The Macquarie River meanders right beside my new home! No wonder that lucerne I munched on was so juicy.

As soon as I got off the horse float, I noticed a dressage arena and a round yard. Wow looks pretty nice. Lovely big green backyard and lots of beautiful trees.

Matthew led me down to the paddock and let me go. Wow lovely green grass! Yes, bring it on!

On the western side of my paddock is another horse, her name is Sophie. She is Lee's horse, a beautiful brown Warmblood with amazing long eyelashes. Then on the eastern side of me, oh my heavens! There are these things, horses, called trotters! They are a bit silly and there's a very bossy gelding in there that gives all the other horses a very hard time. I don't think I like him very much, he's a bit nasty. But I'll make friends with anybody. I'm the new kid on the block.

It didn't take me long to settle in and feel quite at home. I was getting two lovely hard feeds per day, and I was being fed Matthew's homegrown lucerne hay each morning and night, plus a paddock full of grass. What else could a girl want!

But I must say that first afternoon when the Blind Chick came down to feed me, she had a long white cane thing she held out in front of her, tapping it on the ground. What the heck is that! But then I realised she uses the white cane to guide her around the garden and to find her way to my paddock gate, to me. How cool!

After the Blind Chick tips my dinner into my paddock container, she headed back to the tack shed. While I'm eating my hard feed, she washes the feed bucket out then comes back and gives me a biscuit of hay. Yum. While I'm eating this gourmet meal she stands and has a chat with me for a while, giving me lots of pats, and a few more carrots.

I know we're going to get on mighty fine.

Lola

*

THE HORSE

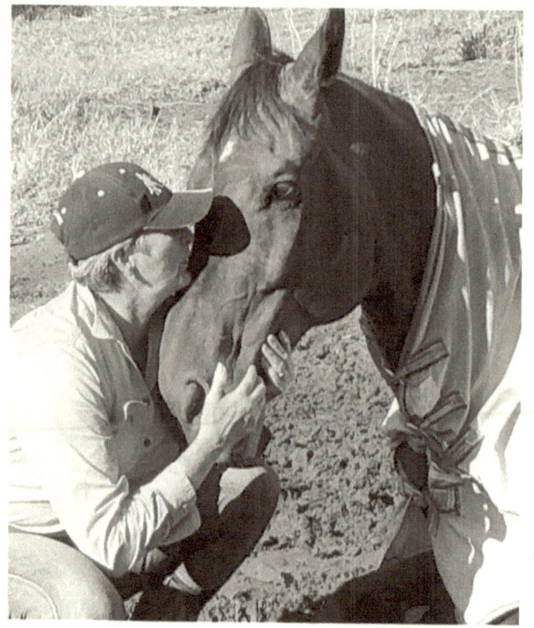

THE HORSE

by Sue-Ellen Lovett

You bring Grace, you bring Beauty.
You bring Love, you bring Assurance.
You love Unconditionally, without Judgement.

Through your eyes life is Simple, Beautiful,
Uncomplicated and oh so Special.

If we could only see through your eyes,
Accept people for who they are and what they are.
All they need to do is look into your eyes,
For the reflection of themselves.

You bring Unconditional Love and Attainable Dreams.
All we have to do is believe, reach out and dream.
With you the dreams come true.

There are lessons to be learned from you
my beautiful friend, my horse.
Learning not to judge, accepting people
for who they are and what they are,
Bringing us back to life, to love unconditionally.

The unconditional love you bring to my life
allows me to Grow and to Believe.
To use my wings and fly, instead of winging it.
So I can soar in the clouds.

I will listen, I will learn to be present,
and I will grow with your help.
I will not listen to the outside influences
that don't know how to listen.
I will learn and do the work,
so we can grow and be as one.

Our ability to fly together starts on the ground.
In time you will learn to trust me, then I'll ride you.
We will soar above the fields on the wind together.

I will learn to trust you as you trust me.
I will learn to trust myself.
I will learn to ask and not tell.
I will learn to be present, to listen,
to feel the love and not to question.

Thank you, my beautiful horse, for bringing
unconditional love, trust, and belief to my life.

With your guidance I will endeavour to be
the best person I can be.
Together we shall work on moving forward,
one beautiful step at a time.

Thank you, my beautiful friend, my horse.

*

IT'S INFECTIOUS

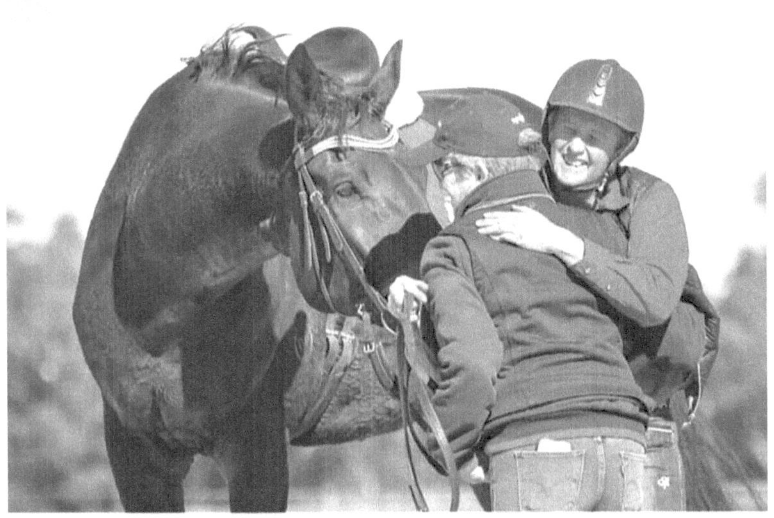

Johno, Cathy Drury-Klien & The Blind Chick   ©2C Photography

Oh my goodness!
I could set my watch by it, if I wore such a device.

Every morning my Blind Chick greets each new day with a Smile. Regardless of how the world is behaving or treating her!

I couldn't help but share with you this poem. You'll be able to understand why it's one of her all time favourites.

SMILE
By Spike Milligan

Smiling is infectious, you catch it like the flu.

When someone smiled at me today, I started smiling too.

I went around the corner, and someone saw my grin.

When he smiled, I realized, I'd passed it on to him.

I thought about that smile, then I realized its worth.

A single smile, just like mine could travel round the earth.

So, if you feel a smile begin, don't leave it undetected.

Let's start an epidemic quick, and get the world infected!

*

A LOT TO LEARN FOR LOLA

The Blind Chick & I

Well, I must say, it has been interesting getting used to the white cane she swings around all the time. It even has bells on it! Yes, not great for my delicate hearing but I'm getting used to it and I get it. The bells frighten the snakes away. We love living beside a river, but so do brown snakes!

At first the ding, ding, ding noisy cane frightened me a little bit, I wondered if she was gonna hit me with it! But I've learnt it's what she uses, she needs, to orientate herself from point A to point B.

The other day the Blind Chick took me up to the tack shed and wow, so much for me to look at, including the inquisitive, rowdy trotters from next door. They run, run, run around a lot, and have a great ability to interrupt other horses, including me and my concentration. But the Blind Chick was very patient, she just kept asking me to lower my head and relax. She gave me a lovely massage with the Equissage machine. This has a big pad that goes on my back which made me feel sooo good afterwards. Plus there's more! Yes, it has a handheld massager as well. This the Blind Chick used on other parts of my body like my legs, that the big pad doesn't get to. It was lovely.

But I was still a little bit upset and a little bit disturbed. Those trotters were running around a lot. Then the Blind Chick took me out to the dressage arena and gave me a little bit of a lunge. This went quite well, mind you I can't say I'm fond of doing circles, but there's not much more you can do on the lunge. The Blind Chick was extremely patient with me, taking the time to talk me through everything.

We did lots and lots and lots and lots of walking to get me relaxed. Then we did some trotting, just nice soft relaxed trot, trying to encourage me to drop my head and relax and stop looking at those trotters!

Really those trotters are a blinking nuisance! They kept running away which upset me quite a bit. And then I wasn't concentrating on what the Blind Chick was asking me to do, so she kept trying to get me to steady and relax back to a walk, and relax back to a walk, and relax. But those trotters, they truly are a pain you know! If they stood around like other horses, it wouldn't be a problem. But they run around like lunatics! It's as if they have ants in their pants.

Now I've got to explain to you how when we are going anywhere from point A to point B, the Blind Chick swings her cane from left to right and back again, out in front of us as we walk. And again, I get it. But every now and again it hits something! Typically it's the base of a tree, but ouch, that could have been her hitting the tree. And yes, sometimes when there's a low branch she does get hit in the face, which must be quite a shock and quite confronting. And that happens because the white cane doesn't cover things up high. How amazing is our Blind Chick. Every day she is doing the best she can.

We come back to the tack shed and I get a brush, a lovely clean rug and taken down to my paddock with the white cane swinging from side to side stopping her from falling into the garden and me following. I'm sure things are going work out fine with us, it'll just take us a little while to get to know each other. And as the Blind Chick's other horse Johno used to say, "Just one step at a time and you never know where you will end up."

With each day it's all getting easier and more familiar. The white cane no longer worries me. Not that it bothered me that much in any case. But it has a job to do, and it helps the Blind Chick find her way around the farm.

The Blind Chick has also got two lovely friends Jacqueline and Jenelle who come out regularly. Jenelle gives her lessons helping to build her confidence and getting to know me. And Jacqueline orientates the Blind Chick by telling her things like when to start turning me because a corner is coming. This is very cool! They work well together the three of them.

Mind you I have arrived with a little bit of baggage. For me some of my previous training was fairly stressful time so I get anxious quite quickly. I'm what you'd call over faced or cooked. Yes, my anxiety level is pretty high. So, the Blind Chick and Jenelle are trying to get me to relax so everything is just soft and quiet. But I want to... rush! Yes, I'm wired to do stuff NOW! Let me canter my brain screams when all I'm expected to do is a nice, relaxed walk. Aaagh! This relaxing gig is a real challenge for me. I've been under the pump, pressured to perform for quite some time. Now I need to learn a different way of moving my body, of thinking. This relaxed new way will take time for me to learn, I'm naturally quite forward, but I want to learn it. I need to learn it!

So, lots of walking and more walking and when I'm asked to do a transition it's so nice. Because that's the thing – It's an ask, not a tell. Its, don't rush Lola. Just take your time Lola. Steady Lola. Whenever I get a little bit worried I automatically go straight into my anxious default mode, which is doing passage, the very elevated and collected trot, which is not needed. Okay, I know that. But it's when I'm feeling anxious. The other thing I can do is jack up or pigroot, and sometimes I do a little rear, which is very naughty. I know, but it's when I get anxious and I don't know, my head has so much in it and I'm trying to work things out and trying to do the right thing. But the Blind Chick just wants me to relax, just relax and take it easy.

I am trying to do my best with the relaxing thing. It's not easy when you have been in a pressure cooker for so long and under so much pressure. But I like it, it feels good when I relax. I just need to let it happen. But I think it's going to take a little time to get out of my system as I am wound up a little bit, like a tight rubber band. I think I need to do what Jenelle is telling the Blind Chick to do and breathe, relax and take a deep breath in. Lucky me that the Blind Chick is in no hurry and she is taking the time it takes to let me learn how to relax and unwind the very tight little rubber band inside of me.

I must say as time goes on; I am really enjoying the training. Okay in the dressage arena it can get a tad boring because this big rectangle sand pit is only 20 metres by 60 metres. But I am slowly learning to relax and canter a circle without jacking up or pig rooting and not anticipating what next movement I'm going to be asked to do. I'm just cantering a circle and I am relaxing and around we go and no pigrooting and back to a walk as a reward. This is cool, I'm liking not having all the pressure.

The Blind Chick has also put me on some amazing products developed by Poseidon Equine. It's called Digestive EQ, which is for my tummy. Because if we have good gut health this will help by leading to less anxiety and less tummy aches and hopefully avoid getting things like stomach ulcers or colic.

I have been on the Digestive EQ for a little while now, and I must say my tummy is not feeling like it's in knots like it used to. I am slowly starting to feel more relaxed. While the Digestive EQ is doing a wonderful job, not having so much pressure put on me is also making everything much easier. I'm so much happier. Less stress, less pressure. Relax and enjoy the ride.

The Blind Chick has also got me on Digestive VM which is a multi-vitamin for horses. So, she really doesn't need to add a lot to my feed as I am also getting Matthews homegrown lucerne hay. I have a very bland diet I must say - Speedy Beet and my additives and some salt. But all of this helps with a healthy gut and a much happier pony.

We have also been down for lessons with an amazing dressage rider who is also a Para-Olympian called Lisa Martin. Oh, my heavens, this was such an experience. I had a lovely big paddock to stay in and lots of other horses neighbouring me, so I was really happy. Until I saw Lisa and the thing with wheels behind a horse. I didn't get what was going on at all. But then I learnt Lisa does carriage driving, with a beautiful little horse called Jimmy. I hadn't seen a horse with wheels behind it before, and I was not impressed.

After I got over my episode of seeing Jimmy with the wheels behind him and Lisa on top of those wheels, things sort of got a little bit back to normal. For our first lesson we started off in the round yard, which was great. It was a little difficult for the Blind Chick in the dressage arena as when she rides at home, we ride of a morning, so she uses the sun for orientation, or she has Jacqueline there orientating her while Jenelle gives her a lesson. Gee-whiz, it would've made it much easier if she just thought of this with Lisa as she had absolutely no idea where she was at any time in the arena. So Lisa had to do double the work as far as do the instructing and orientation. Then the next day the Blind Chick remembered oh my heavens Anita is with us. "Anita could be the living markers and call me from place to place." Oh, my heavens this made the world of difference to the Blind Chick's orientation. We were now able to do straight lines which made it so much easier for setting up movements.

I was still having a little issue with my anxiety and wanting to jack up and suck back, but Lisa made the Blind Chick ride me more forward, more forward into an extended canter.

Sucking back is when the horse sort of hangs back, they're reluctant to go forward. Which was me!

Holy cow I think the Blind Chick was hanging on with both butt cheeks because she was being pushed way out of her comfort zone! And I had to work a little harder and think about what I was doing every time I was wanting to jack up or be a little naughty. But this riding me forward did the job, in fact it did numerous jobs. It stopped my jacking up, but it also gave the Blind Chick the confidence to keep riding me forward. She'd been a little afraid of what I might have been going to do, keeping in mind she has not been riding me long and... she is totally blind.

I suspect confidence is a real issue when you can't see. You really do have to put a lot of trust in the horse, and I must say I am still dealing with some of my own issues with the anxiety, the stress and the tension. So, I'm sure we will eventually sort all of this out, but it will take the time it takes.

I must say I think the Blind Chick was pretty impressed after her lessons with Lisa because there was a new found confidence. Yippee, now the Blind Chick has started riding me at home with no one there watching or coaching us. Which was very cool. I still had my odd little anxiety attacks, and had the odd pigroot and jack up and sometimes I would be really naughty and do a bit of a rear, but I am slowly getting out of all of those bad habits and things are definitely on the improve.

But I'm only improving because the Blind Chick has structured my training to be no pressure, no tricks, just keeping it very basic. There's always lots of walking, trotting, extended trot, collected trot, lots of transitions into the canter, extended canter, collected canter and extended canter back to the trot. Lots and lots of transitions. But it's all being done very relaxed. We do a little bit of leg yielding, and a little bit of shoulder in. But none of the tricks, no flying changes, no pirouettes, no half passes, just keeping it simple. No pressure.

So, this has totally paid off because now when we go riding it is so cool, I am feeling so much better in myself. We are looking at 10 months down the track now, wow how those months have flown, and I can go out freely and enjoy the ride. I no longer feel as if I'm a wound-up rubber band. But it takes the time it takes, and the Blind Chick has given me that time. We are in no hurry. We have lots of goals, but again, it will be one step at a time.

I know one of the Blind Chick's' goals is to get back doing dressage. Hopefully with Covid settling down we'll get back to having lessons with Lisa and concentrate on our dressage. But what we are doing at home is wonderful and the Blind Chick doesn't have that white cane anymore, she has a new Guide Dog, his name is Woody.

It's been rather lovely watching the Blind Chick train with Woody. Watching their destination work and them walking down to my paddock together, is very interesting. He sits and she gives him a treat and lots of pats and after day three they came down to my paddock and I came up to the gate to get some carrots, of course. And the Blind Chick asked Woody to sit outside the gate, and she came in with a halter and caught me. Then Woody lead the Blind Chick and I up to the tack shed and she gave me a big brush. Then Danni, her Guide Dog trainer led me out to the dressage arena. Then the Blind Chick, Woody and I started our stuff. Woody leading us around the arena. This was very cool! And the Blind Chick was very excited!

So, I'm guessing there are going to be loads of adventures with my good self, Lola, with the wonderful Guide Dog Woody and the Blind Chick.

Your friend

Woody

Guide Dog Extraordinaire

*

QUESTIONS PEOPLE HAVE ASKED ME

©Guide Dogs NSW

WHAT DID YOU DO WHEN YOU WERE BEING PUPPY WALKED? DID YOU LEARN ANYTHING, OR WERE YOU JUST ON HOLIDAY?

No, the walking really wasn't a holiday. As much as it was lots of fun, it was also a big learning experience. It gave me time to grow up before I went and started my Guide Dog training.

I learnt lots of wonderful things when I was being puppy walked. I learnt how to walk on a lead, that trying to chase the neighbour's cat wasn't ok, that sitting, stopping, and having manners was ok. I even learnt to sit and shake hands before I started eating my dinner. These were all some of the little things I learnt early on, that would help the Guide Dogs Trainers when they start training me.

HOW LONG DID YOU PUPPY WALK FOR?

I was puppy walked for 16 months and enjoyed every minute of it. Mind you, I think I was a little bit rambunctious. I was like a little kid, I just needed to have direction and things to do all the time.

WHAT IS WEARING THE HARNESS LIKE?
HOW DOES IT GO ON? HOW DOES IT WORK?

My harness is made of leather, it has a lovely soft strap around my chest and one over my belly and back, like a girth. It's all super soft leather.

It gets eased over my head and does up with a clip around my belly. The girth bit is adjustable, which is handy in case I put on some weight. Plus, I need that adjustability because I'm not fully grown yet.

When the Blind Chick has me guiding her, she stands at my shoulder, picks up the handle and gives me the command to walk on. "Up up" she says, which is Guide Dog speak for 'Walk On'.

The Blind Chick feels the connection to me through the handle of the harness. I feel the harness as slight pressure on my chest, as I stride forward guiding her wherever we need to go.

DID YOU ENJOY YOUR GUIDE DOG TRAINING?
WHAT WERE SOME OF THE HIGHLIGHTS?

Oh yes, I certainly enjoyed my Guide Dog training. It was really interesting. This is where I learnt that I had such a very important job to guide people around. As my training progressed, the importance of what I'd be doing sunk in more and more. Being the eyes for blind and visually impaired people is a massive responsibility.

With my training I learnt to stop at the curb and wait for cars to go past. In the city where I trained, we had traffic lights, so we'd listen for the beep, beep, beep, beep, then walk across. But while I was learning about all these weird sounds and when to walk on, or not, it was the Guide Dog handler that made those go or not go decisions, not me.

But once I graduate, knowing all the things I need to, when I'm with my blind person I will sometimes need to make those go or not go decision.

If for example, my blind person makes the wrong decision, like if they ask me to start walking across the pedestrian crossing, but I see a car coming, I will gently guide myself in front of their legs and stop them from walking any further. I don't want them walking in front of a vehicle. Whoohoo, and guess what? There aren't any traffic lights on the farm!   I've been given someone's life to protect, yes, that's so much responsibility for one golden Labrador. Hence why I take my job so very seriously.

We also learnt about not talking to other dogs when we're working, which is anytime our harness is on.

This is a really tough one. I admit to how difficult it is to zone out when people try and talk to me, pat me, or feed me, when I'm working. It's really important for me to keep my blind person safe and going where we are supposed to be going. I can't let a random person or persons distracting me.

When my harness is on, I'm working. So please, leave me to do my job.

Getting trained to be a Guide Dog is a real team effort, lots of people are involved. But for me the main trainer was a lovely man called Thomas.

DID PEOPLE TRY TO FEED YOU WHILE YOU WERE IN HARNESS BEING TRAINED?

Oh yes, they certainly did. Who doesn't want to feed a cute dog! But my Guide Dog trainer Tom, was very quick to point out to people that I was a working dog, and while the harness was on me it is really important that I don't get distracted by food or by someone calling out to me. Him explaining this was very, very good for public awareness.

DID YOU GO ON TRAINS AND
LEARN TO GO IN CARS?

Oh yes, this was an important part of my training. I went on a train, I sat at Tom's feet underneath the seat the entire time. It was a really weird experience going on a train with all the clickety-clackety, but it was quite mesmerising. If I remember rightly, I fell asleep.

As for travelling in cars, yes, I often travel in the back of the car, but I also sit at the foot of my person. Given I'm quite a leggy large dog, I would never be asked to travel in the footwell on long distances.

YOU HAD SIX PUPPIES IN YOUR LITTER, ARE ANY
OF YOUR BROTHERS AND SISTERS GUIDE DOGS?

Oh heavens yes! We are quite an amazing family. Two of my siblings are Guide Dogs, so that's three out of six from one litter as Guide Dogs. A sister is a Therapy Dog, and the two remaining siblings went interstate. I'm not sure what they're up to, but I am sure they're doing a great job whatever it is. I am very proud of my family.

DID YOU LIKE THE MOVE TO LIVING ON A FARM?

Oh yes, wow, wow and wow! Being a farm boy is wonderful! There are loads of places to run and play when I'm let free. I get to do amazing things like go out with Matthew and my Blind Chick on the motorbike, following them around the paddock while they check crops or fences. It is so much fun. They even have a tandem pushbike that I love running along beside when they go for a cycle.

DO YOU HAVE ANY OTHER
FRIENDS ON THE FARM?

Definitely, especially our next-door neighbours. Lee and John are Matthew's mum and dad, they have a lovely little caboodle called Bonnie. She comes and says hello to me each day. Sometimes she'll even sit on the veranda with me.

Then there is Lola, the lovely black horse. She is very cool; I enjoy hanging out with her and guiding her and the Blind Chick to the dressage arena to train. That's loads of fun!

Then there is Thunder Paws, the Blind Chick's pussycat. He took a little while to warm to me, but we are pretty good mates now.

DO YOU GO FOR WALKS WITH
YOUR BLIND CHICK?

Yes, we certainly do. We go for some lovely long walks. I've learnt a lot of new destinations since being on the farm.

It is also lovely to go on walks with Matthew and the Blind Chick out to check Matthew's crops. This year he has lupins growing, they're growing really well. I think he will be harvesting probably in December, and I might get to go in the harvester. That'll be very, very exciting.

DO YOU GET TO INTERACT
WITH A LOT OF PEOPLE?

No not really. Matthew toilets me each evening and I mainly work with my Blind Chick. It's important when you are a working dog that your focus is on your owner. I admit that I quite like it that way. Mind you, I am a little bit of a social butterfly. I like watching on when we go somewhere, or visitors come to the farm.

WAS LEARNING TO BE A GUIDE DOG EASY?

No, not really. I was a very busy Guide Dog in training. Being such an enthusiastic character, meant I need to be doing things all the time. Yes, sometimes I was a bit of the class clown, but I still passed all my Guide Dog tests with flying colours. I love my job as a Guide Dog. I truly believe it's in my DNA to do this job. I was born to lead. I was born to spend my life looking after my Blind Chick, Sue Ellen.

Your friend

Woody

Guide Dog Extraordinaire

*

A DAY IN MY LIFE

Meeting Lola for the first time

You may ask – "What is it like being Guide Dog Woody?"
So here goes, this is what my average day is like. Welcome to my world.

The alarm goes off at 6 am, there's movement at the station! My Blind Chick is up and gets Matthew's breakfast while I wait patiently for my turn.

Then she comes and gets me from the laundry where I am comfortably ensconced on my deliciously soft bed that's especially lovely is winter with the warmth from the wood fire, mind you I do have a very thick coat and I do lose a lot of hair. Oopsie!

First things first though, I need to be toileted. This is not done in the harness as I am very clever and we have a routine. My Blind Chick comes in and puts the lead on me, then we walk outside and I sit at the top of the veranda steps. My Blind Chick then says, "walk on Woody" and I slowly go down the steps, one step at a time, keeping in mind I have no harness on while I'm doing this.

I guide my Blind Chick through the garden, through the Pine trees, out to the front yard. The command for doing my toileting is "quick, quick" and because I'm so obedient, I quickly do my business. Once that's done, I return and sit quietly at the left side of my Blind Chick, waiting for my next command.

Gee, some of the smells of a morning are pretty amazing. We have a local fox that sometimes comes around and leaves their terrible stink in the yard. I love the frosty foggy mornings here, they're so crisp and beautiful.

Oops, back to our routine.

My Blind Chick gives the command "inside Woody, inside" and off we go back through the Pine trees to the house. Don't forget I am really clever, I'm doing all of this without a harness on. Once through the Pine trees I stop at the bottom of the veranda stairs and wait for my Blind Chick to feel with her foot where we are. Then she says, "forward Woody" and I walk slowly up the stairs one at a time.

We then quietly walk around to the front of the house, to where my kennel is during winter. Why there? Because the sun comes up on the northern side of the house and it's warmer and really lovely out front. When we get to my kennel I stop, she takes my lead off and clips a chain on me. I then lie on my mat in the sun and enjoy the spectacular morning. It really is beautiful here.

My Blind Chick goes off and does whatever she needs to do. When she returns, she has my harness with her. I have to admit I do love it when I see her with my harness. It's made of really soft leather and fits comfortably around my chest and around my waist. There's a handle that comes up through the harness on my back that my Blind Chick holds onto. It's via that handle that I guide her.

When the harness appears, this means I've got work to do!

While she puts my harness on, I sit quietly on her left-hand side. She clips my lead on, then puts the chest part of the harness on, she checks it's the right way around and the handle isn't on my nose, hee hee. She puts the strap around my belly in a way that's sort of equivalent to putting a girth on a horse. Sometimes when I was younger, I admit, I really struggled to sit quietly while

being harnessed. I was so excited to be working that I'd fidget...
a lot! I don't do that now. But just because you see me sitting
quietly, don't take that as me not bursting with excitement inside.
Given how being part of my new family and life here on the farm
is never dull, I don't imagine my excitement to be working will
ever dull. Even when I'm older and have mastered all there is
about being my Blind Chicks best Guide Dog EVER, I'll still be
excited when I'm being harnessed.

With the harness being such lovely soft leather it's really quite
comfortable to wear. The handle my Blind Chick holds in her left
hand is also made a leather, but it has a piece of wire inside it.
That wire keeps it the shape it needs to be and quite rigid.

How lucky am I to be looked after so well. My harness leather
smells so nice all the time because guess who oils it routinely, so
it stays lovely and soft.

Ok, it's time to go and yes, I'm busting with excitement. We're
off to do some jobs. My Blind Chick askes me to "up, stand" and
then she says the words I've been sooo waiting for – "walk on
Woody, find the stairs". I walk to the stairs and stop at the top so
we can then walk down them together, one stairs one at a time.

It is important that you realise how much I love my job and
how much responsibility is involved in me being a Guide Dog. I
have to do everything SLOWLY and QUIETLY. When it comes to
going up or down steps this is must be done one step at a time, no
rushing or pulling. I could easily make my Blind Chick fall, which
would be horrible.

After we go down the steps the first command is "to Lola's
paddock Woody, Lola's paddock." So off I go walking confidently
down through the garden to Lola's paddock. We then go and get
some hay and feed it to Lola. This is always good fun as she is one
of my mates and I love the smell of the horse. Typically, we say
hello to each other by touch noses. Often our Blind Chick gives
Lola a carrot and me a treat for being such a good boy.

Then my Blind Chick asks me to guide her back to the tack shed.
Oh, guess where we go next? Yippee I learnt a new destination

a week or so ago, which is Veggie Garden. So off we go to the veggie garden. Here she waters the plants and has a feel of how well everything is growing. Gosh the earth smells so lovely.

After doing the veggie garden we go for a walk down to the front gate which is about a kilometre from the house. So, one kilometre there and back. This is our number one great exercise and there are lots of smells along the way. But being a Guide Dog I've had to learn, and am still perfecting it, to take no notice of the smells. Yes, it's not easy. But each day I give it my best shot and just keep walk on and looking after my Blind Chick.

Yes, keep in mind dogs have a very keen sense of smell and sometimes it's extremely difficult not to keep sniffing. But I don't, I'm a very good guy dog.

Being on a farm is a lot different from the training I did when I was doing my Guide Dog training in the city. Yes there were lots more traffic lights, cars and other things, but the farm is very different. Here we have mainly destination work to do, not lots of cars, trucks, buses, and people to avoid work.

Hopefully you can tell how much I love my life here on the farm.

Some days I take my Blind Chick down to find Lola in the paddock. This is always cool fun because Lola is not always in the same place. But I know the command "find Lola Woody" and I'm really good at it.

Wow in that horse paddock there are lots of stuff I would like to smell and probably chew or eat. Dogs love horse poo! But my Blind Chick has educated me that horse poo will never been on my menu. I'm not allowed to eat it.

After I lead my Blind Chick and Lola up to the gate leading out of Lola's paddock, there's a big ledge which I stop at. Once my Blind Chick has found the ledge, she steps up and says "good boy Woody, to the tack shed." I lead Lola and my Blind Chick to the tack shed but as I walk I feel the lovely soft grass under my feet. Hmm, it's even a little damp from the early morning frost.

Did you know that some Guide Dogs are allergic to grass on their feet! Yes. They get allergies and will chew at their toes.

Thank heavens I don't have that as we do a lot of work on the grass.

Oh how funny, there's something I just noticed out the corner of my eye. It's fluffy and seems to think I haven't noticed him. Go Thunder Paws, the largest furball I've ever met. He thinks my Blind Chick and I work really well together. He told me he used to be very frightened of me, when I first arrived and was so big and had a long wiggly tail. But now he is much more confident in my presence. I probably would still like to chase him, but I know that's not allowed.

Now there's another thing that's not negotiable about being a Guide Dog I need to tell you about. And it's a biggie. It's called dog distraction! Yes, on our the farm we not only have me, we also have Matthew's mum and dad's dog, they live next door. Lee and John have a caboodle called Bonnie.

But you've got to give her points for trying. In those early weeks she'd come and say hello to me, but I'd ignore her every time if I had the harnesses on. It's critical when I'm working that my full attention is on my Blind Chick and what we are doing. I probably wouldn't really play with Bonnie anyway, even if I wasn't in harness. Why? Because she's quite small and as you know I'm rather large. I could ball her over and hurt her without intending too of course.

The other thing that happens when I'm not working and I'm sitting at my kennel is Matthew sometimes comes and clips my toenails. This happens probably once a month. I don't mind this being done at all. He just does one at a time while I lie there quietly. It doesn't hurt.

Oops, back to what my day is like.

Once we're finished doing whatever we've been doing around the property, at the garden or with Lola, my Blind Chick says "to the house Woody, to the house" and I guide her to the bottom step that leads up onto the veranda. She then gives me the command to "walk on" and up we go, one step at a time. If it's towards the end of the day, we'll stop outside the laundry door and I sit quietly while she gently takes my harness off and hangs it on the hat peg.

I then guide my Blind Chick around the veranda to my kennel where I'm tied up and can have some downtime to relax. I get a tad excited though around about 3 pm, my dinner time! I get my dog biscuits and every Monday I get an egg with my dog biscuits. I also get fish oil tablets each day to help my coat be lovely and shiny.

For my teeth I have a bone called a Nylabone, this I chew on during the day when ever I like. It helps keep the plaque off my teeth, so they stay nice and white and bright.

You know it is a pretty cool gig being a Guide Dog. Especially a Guide Dog on a farm. There are so many more things to see and do than when I lived in the city. So many more things to smell and look at. I often see the odd fox running across the lawn or a bunny rabbit hopping around the garden. I think I could probably chase that bunny rabbit and catch it. That would be cool fun. But I generally only see them when I'm sitting on the veranda having some downtime.

The other thing I thought I'd mention is all of the wonderful things I pick up from my Blind Chick when we are working. I pick up on her emotions, I can sense when she is sad or stressed. I pick this all up and I just gently touch my nose on her leg to let her know everything is okay, I'm looking after her. As a Guide Dog we pick up so many extra things that people don't realise. The other biggie I pick up on is if she is anxious. Living next to the river is lovely but it comes with something that scares my Blind Chick. Snakes! I know she always worries about them, she's stepped on them in the past. So, with the combination of living by the river, which they love and summer time having them be out and about a lot more, we make sure we make enough noise when we're moving around the garden and around the farm to hopefully deter the snakes and get them to move along.

If you're wondering if I've done anything naughty since being on the farm well.. maybe! Just the odd one or two little things. One was I devoured my Blind Chick's sunglasses. No excuse that I was young and still learning. They were irreparable. Ooops. While tying me up she dropped them and felt everywhere looking for them. Then light bulb moment, she decided to check what I had stashed in my kennel. Oopsie! I'd eaten or chewed nearly every part of them. She picked up the little remnants and put them in the bin. From then on because I'm such a chewer, I always have a Nylabone handy to keep me occupied.

Like I said earlier, Guide Dogs, well all dogs, have a great sense of smell. It's not just my Blind Chick who might toilet me, very often it's Matthew. Ooops one day when I was off with Matthew in the front yard, guess what Lola had left there? Yes, a large manure. Guess who found it and thought it was Candy? I grabbed a couple of manure nuggets and ran off eating them. Oh they were scrumptious. Ooops my Blind Chick and Matthew were not impressed. But hey, I'm a dog and we love smelly things to eat if we get the chance. Don't forget, first and foremost I am a dog.

I'm so looking forward to summer as ' baths me every couple of weeks. This is always great fun when she soaps me up, I shake like crazy and put soap all over her. Then when she rinses me guess what I do. Yes, I shake again and put water all over her! I think she ends up just as wet as I am. I always smell lovely after bath time.

The other thing I thought I'd mention is my hearing. It is so good I know where my Blind Chick is at all times, especially when she's using her white cane. The cane isn't just to help her not bang into things, it has a bell on it for two reasons. Firstly, to deter the snakes and secondly when Lola hears the bell approaching, even as soon as us going down the veranda steps, she whinnies out to us, letting us know she knows my Blind Chick is coming to feed her. My sense of hearing is quite amazing. Being so I'm not a fan of loud noises like guns going off, fireworks or things like that. Thank heavens those things don't happen here on the farm.

I extra love it when my day includes going for a run with Matthew and my Blind Chick. I run beside them when they're on the tandem pushbike or on the motorbike, this is always loads of fun. We can go very fast with the motorbike, but I know not to run in front of it. I just run along the side with my mate my Blind Chick next to me. There is no harness, no lead. I am free to do as much sniffing as I like. Lucky me.

I hope you enjoyed spending this typical day in my life with me.

Your friend

Woody

Guide Dog Extraordinaire

*

WOODY'S TRAINING JOURNAL

We thought you'd like to come join us and take a deep dive into what it takes to train a Guide Dog.

Welcome to the critical first 14 days of Woody's training when he first arrived at the farm in Dubbo to guide me, his Blind Chick.

*

DAY 1 – HE'S HERE, HE'S HERE!

Welcome Woody. What a difference a Guide Dog makes!

Woohoo! Woody, my new Guide Dog has arrived!

Well, it was going to be an extremely busy day today; a riding lesson this morning and then Woody arriving this afternoon. But no! It rained last night quite a lot, so the dressage arena was in flood. I had to cancel todays riding lesson which gave me the opportunity to do a few more domestic goddess duties like washing and getting things organised for Woody's arrival.

I finished organising his kennel on the front veranda. Lucky Woody actually has two kennels; the one on the veranda plus one next to the dressage arena. The latter he can sit in, in the shade, while I have a ride on Lola.

He's here! He's here!

Oh wow, it was super cool when Woody arrived. Danni my Guide Dog trainer said when they turned up our driveway, Woody stood up! She said that it was the first and only time he had stood during the whole trip. He must've known where he was. I thought that was very cool!

When Danni and Woody arrived, I went out to greet them using my trusty white cane. Yippee, that's about to be retired. Ha Ha. I took Woody while Danni brought all of his goodies inside. Then we had a little break and sat on the veranda and chatted. Woody settled down and sat between my legs. He was quite content from the start, which was really lovely. It felt like he and I was meant to be.

When we put him on his mat on the veranda with a big bucket of water, the first thing he did was put his nose into the water and blow bubbles! Then he started pawing the water out of the bucket with his feet. He nearly emptied the whole bucket! He was playing like a kid. It was hilarious.

I then fed him. I went and got his dog biscuits with my white cane and came back up the steps. I asked Woody to sit and shake hands. I told him he has lovely manners, which is very cool. After Danni drove away, Woody and I went for a walk out into the garden and sat under the Polonia tree. I gave him a big brush and we just sat and had a chat, spending some quality time together. There was to be no work today. It was way too hot, and he had had a big day travelling for hours to come here.

I am so chuffed. Woody is super laid-back and seems so happy and content. I settled him in the laundry, where he will spend each evening, or if the weather was to bad for him to be on the veranda. This is a great spot for him because he gets to benefit from the air conditioning. He's really happy, he's sitting in there chewing on a bone.

Phew, I'm so relieved! It is always a worry when you get a new dog that they are content, happy and relaxed around you and that they feel comfortable in the new environment, their new home. Thankfully Woody seems very relaxed and happy indeed.

So tomorrow morning, bring it on, Woody and I start our training. We will do some destination work, but firstly, we'll fit his harness. The handle on his harness is the link to me, that's how we communicate. That's what our training will do a lot of.

Thunder Paws our beautiful pussycat has not met Woody yet. This could be interesting...

I can't wait for tomorrow to come and our training to begin. We will possibly do a walk to the front gate first, then start doing the destination work. Teaching Woody different destinations, whether it be the dressage arena, the tack shed or down to Lola. I would like to eventually teach Woody to 'find Lola' in the paddock, but this will come further down the track.

I am so looking forward to not getting lost in the garden! Life not getting lost will be wonderful.

*

DAY 2 – MY CONFIDENCE HAS TAKEN A GIANT LEAP

Mobility & Independence – Thank you Woody

Wow, wow, wow and wow! What an amazing morning. I would be telling a fib to say I wasn't excited to start training with Woody this morning. I was up really early, got all of my domestic goddess duties done, fed Lola and took Woody for a walk outside to do his toiletries. Even doing that he was a total legend. He led me back inside without the harness on! What a clever boy and this is only the start of our second day together!

When Danni arrived, we fitted Woody's harness and then worked out a handle that was going to the right length for me. Our first destination was "Tack Shed", which meant Woody had to guide me from the house, down the steps, and out to the tack shed.

Well look out! This dog is a legend! Straight to the tack shed and then he guided me perfectly on the return trip back to the house. When he got to the veranda steps, he took one step at a time, up the steps. Wow, he is learning so quickly!

But okay I'm a bit excited and I am getting ahead of myself! We firstly went for a walk to the front gate, which is a kilometre down and a kilometre back. Woody did not miss a beat. We had a wonderful walk down to the gate and back and guess what! I didn't get lost coming back through the garden! I was so excited. It was too cool! Woody just quietly took me through the garden, did a right turn, then another right turn, and I couldn't resist – I asked him to go to the tack shed, and straight to the tack shed he went. Oh my lord, this is so cool.

Of course I gave him a treat and a big cuddle to reward him.

Then it was time for some more destination work - down to Lola's paddock. Well, when we got down there Lola came to see us and oops, I'd forgotten to take a carrot. I felt so bad! Lola and Woody had a chat for a while. It was just so nice, Woody loves Lola, and Lola doesn't seem to mind Woody, phew, that's wonderful. Maybe in the next two days I will have a go at Woody leading Lola and I? Yes, exciting times ahead.

After having a chat with Lola, Woody guided me back through the garden, to the tack shed and straight to its door. What a legend of a dog. I cannot tell you how excited I was this morning to start my training. But what I'm feeling now, oh, I cannot explain it. The independence and mobility that my Guide Dog gives me is, oh my heavens, totally amazing! It's life changing. It is so nice to be able to go through the garden and know I'm not going to get lost, or injured on a low hanging branch or prickly tree!

After we returned to the house we sat on the veranda for a little while to give Woody a rest and some water. Then we were off, to the dressage arena. On the walk to the dressage arena, I held Danni's arm so we could orientate Woody to that new destination "to the dressage arena Woody, to the dressage arena." He has done this route once before when he visited mid-December last year. At that time we used the mark of where he had to go as "the mounting block."

Well guess what? As we came around the round yard I said, "to the mounting block Woody, to the mounting block," and even though I just had his lead, not his Guide Dog harness, he took me straight to the mounting block! What an incredible dog. Woody also loved his lovely new kennel that Matthew built for the end of the dressage arena. I painted it and Matthew put WOODY on it. Danni said it looked really awesome.

I then thought we would have a go at Woody guiding me back through the garden to the tack shed. He hesitated a little bit when we got closer to the tack shed because he hadn't done that route before, but he nailed it. Danni just walked in front of us, and he went, yeah got it, "to the tack shed." He went around Danni and straight to the tack shed. It was another, oh my gosh moment!

What an amazing morning. I have my wings now, and I'm not going to get lost in the garden, and no more encounters with that lemon tree and its prickles!

*

DAY 3 – WHAT A DIFFERENCE A ...

As the saying goes, "What a difference a day makes!" Well, what a difference a Guide Dog makes!

I am so grateful and blessed to have this amazing Guide Dog Woody working with me. We are having a ball. So grateful to our wonderful Guide Dog trainer Danni who is truly amazing and encouraging and she also loves horses, woohoo we rock together!

Today we did another training session down to the front gate and back. Woody did not miss a beat. Danni also got some video footage of us going to the gate which is really cool. When we came home Woody guided me straight back to the house, stopped at the bottom of the steps, then up onto the veranda and onto his mat we went.

Oh my heavens, he learns so quickly. His destination work is truly amazing!

Danni and I then gave him a bit of a break while we chatted about what we would do next. We thought best would be some more destination work. This time it was "to the tack shed" and down to "find Lola."

It was so cool, no help from Danni today! Woody quietly took me to the edge of the veranda where the steps to go down are. Then he guided me down, one step at a time. Then he proceeded to take me to the tack shed, perfectly. Wow, he got a big pat and lots of "good boy." In case you've forgotten, in case I haven't said it enough, Woody is totally awesome!

The next destination was from the tack shed down to Lola through the garden. Wow! Woody rocked it! Straight down to Lola's gate, we stood at the gate and called our beautiful Lola, and obviously given how much she loves carrots, she came to the gate for a treat and a pat straight away.

Lola and Woody had a nice quiet chat together and some downtime. I can see this is going to be so cool when we get Woody leading Lola and I. Neither of them are worried about each other. Maybe, depending on what Danni wants to do tomorrow, maybe tomorrow we might have a go at that?

I'm just so wrapped with how Woody is settling in, with everything!

Then we went back to the tack shed and out to the dressage arena, using the mounting block as the destination. Woody nailed it again. I then asked him to take me to his Woody house, he went straight over to the Woody house and in he went. Oh my heavens, he is just so wonderful and such a good boy.

Then Danni amped things up, she suggested a car trip! We were going into town to have a cuppa. I excitedly rang my wonderful mother-in-law Lee, to see where she would suggest would be a great place for our first outing. Lee suggested a lovely coffee shop in town called Alchemy. So, into the car went Woody and I, and off to town we went. When we arrived we got Woody out of the car and I put him in his harness. He then guided me, following Danni, into the coffee shop.

We got into an area where we were to be seated, so I asked Woody to "find a chair." He did exactly that, I sat down, and Woody proceeded to do what all Guide Dogs should in such situations, he sat at the back of my chair and stayed there, being nice and quiet. Danni and I enjoyed a cuppa and a smashed avocado.

Oh my heavens, it was delicious! While we were sitting chatting Woody slept, he took no notice of the comings and goings of the waitress or the people in the restaurant. It was a wonderful experience. I have another outing on the run sheet for tomorrow. Hmm, maybe we'll find another smashed avocado that tastes even better.

Woohoo! Bring it on! Everything about this outing made my confidence soar. Plus the staff were wonderful.

So, another amazing day training with Woody! This afternoon Danni is coming back out to do some more obedience work. Yesterday we did obedience work on the veranda and Woody was truly awesome. I would get him to sit, and then I would walk away and then come back. The next time I would walk a little bit, get him to sit, then I walk away and then call him to come to me. I love the obedience work, and Woody was just totally awesome.

Words can't describe how I'm feeling about Woody being my guide. Everything is feeling so perfect! You know when you are waiting for the bubble to bust, you keep blowing into it, but it just keeps getting bigger and bigger and brighter. Woody totally rocks.

So yes! I'm loving my training with the beautiful Woody. I am so grateful to Guide Dogs for giving me the opportunity to have another Guide Dog, Woody being my seventh. I forgot how amazing this independence and mobility is, the freedom a Guide Dog provides me. It is life changing. It is totally awesome.

DAY 4 – WOW, WOW AND WOW!

Just one Step at a Time

Woohoo! Wow! This is what it's all about. Oh my heavens I am so loving the training with wonderful Woody. He is such a pleasure. He is such an amazing Guide Dog. I am loving this journey.

Yesterday evening Danni came out and we did obedience work with him on the grass out the front of the house. We just started off with little things, like getting him to sit and stay. I would walk away and then come back, clip on his lead and go for another walk. Halt, sit, undo the lead, walk away, and then call him. His recall was amazing! He came straight to me and sat. I rewarded him with a little treat. His obedience work is wonderful.

Off to the garden we went. We walked around the garden with Danni as my sighted guide, I just held her arm and Woody poked around with us, never going far away. Him not pinging off or even straying a little, made me feel really good. He must like being in our company.

Thunder paws our pussycat is now starting to accept Woody's presence in our house. He now walks past the laundry door and doesn't worry. He even went out with Matthew to toilet Woody last night, which I thought was rather wonderful. Just keeping an eye on that big dog, he was.

This morning we got off to a wonderful start, a walk down to the front gate and back. Two kilometres and Woody did not miss a beat. I love this walk, it's great for the mind and spirit. It was also very cool today, Danni set a few tasks for Woody and I to do by ourselves without her being there to watch us. These helped make sure everything was going well, we did them perfectly. He is such a good boy.

Now this is where it gets exciting. After we returned from our walk to the front gate we went to the tack shed. Then I asked Woody to walk down to Lola's paddock. As I said the destination, off he went. Yes, in case I haven't said it enough, his destination work is amazing. When we reached the gate, Danni got Lola's halter and went and caught Lola. Woody and I walked back to the tack shed and I sat him at the drum at the left-hand side of my tack shed. I asked him to sit and lay down, which he did.

Danni brought Lola up to the tack shed. I took her rug off and gave Lola a brush. Danni and I stood and talked for a little while, while Woody just lay there taking it all in. He did not move. He was such a good boy.

Then Woody and I walked out to the dressage arena, followed by Danni leading Lola. Woody you are a Superstar! Again, he went straight to the mounting block. Perfect, and leading all the way, no hesitation. He knew exactly where we were going.

I taught Woody a new word today, "into the arena." Danni had already led Lola into the arena and was standing beside her. I walked up to Danni's left side, we stood and talked for a little while, Woody sat. Then the four of us quietly walked around the dressage arena on the right rein, which meant Woody was on the outside edge of the dressage arena. This was so cool. Lola took no notice of Woody, and Woody did a wonderful job of guiding. Having Lola there didn't phase him at all.

We got back to the gate, and I asked Danni if we could amp it up a little. "Is it okay if Woody and I take a turn at leading Lola?"

Well! This is where it gets extra exciting! Danni gave me Lola's lead, I had Woody in my left hand, Lola in my right. And I quietly said to Woody, "up, stand, and walk on." Then voila, all three of us were walking around the outside of the arena.

I wish you could see the huge smile on my face while I am dictating these words into my iPhone, and the tears. What happened, in that moment, was pure magic!

This is what having a Guide Dog is all about. My independence, my mobility, my freedom. I can now lead my pony with my Guide Dog. Look out! We are on fire! I'm feeling amazing.

We did a couple of halts along the long side of the arena, getting Woody to stop and Lola to stand quietly. Then I asked Woody to "walk on" and as if he'd done it each day of his life, he lead Lola and I around the arena.

Oh my heavens! How can hee be this brilliant. Woody was so good, and Lola was amazing as well. Being part of this trio felt so darn good.

We did a few exercises with Woody leading Lola and I, then I taught Woody to go to the round yard gate, which he did. He stopped at the round yard gate, I gave Lola back to Danni, and Woody and I walked back around the round yard and over to the tack shed. Danni and Lola followed. I took Woody to his drum, where he sat and lay down while I put a new rug on Lola and gave her a brush and a couple of carrots.

Oh my heavens, today has been magical and amazing!

Then Woody and I walked back down to Lola's paddock, with Danni lead Lola. Yes, it's handy Danni is a horsy chick. Tomorrow I will be leading Lola up from her paddock to the tack shed, and then maybe even out to the dressage arena. But it is all just as our beautiful Johno used to say, one step at a time. And oh, my heavens look where we are doing exactly that - just doing one step at a time.

We then sat in the garden and had a chat for a little while. Then it was time for Danni to get her car so we could do another outing. Alchemy café in Dubbo, here we come!

Oh my heavens it is so lovely going there. The staff are amazing, they brought Woody out a bowl of water with ice cubes in it, which he loved. Danni and I enjoyed another smashed avocado. Again it was beautiful, I couldn't fault it.

While we were at the cafe, we were joined by my wonderful next-door neighbour Noni and her beautiful daughter Sarah. This was wonderful for Woody. People joining us at the café, the comings, and goings, interacting with different people, is all wonderful for his socialisation. He was such a good boy.

Then it was home time. Once we arrived home Woody went straight onto the veranda to relax, and I went inside to do some domestic goddess duties.

DAY 5 – GUESS WHO WENT SOLO?

Moving Forward

First solo walk! Woohoo!

It was an early start again this morning. We had a special job to do today. Woody and I were walking to the gate together without our Guide Dog trainer Danni.

Today was our first solo walk! No pressure.

So, firstly I toileted Woody, completed a couple of domestic goddess duties then put his harness on him. I asked Woody to "up, stand and walk to the stairs." Once there he guided me down them, one step at a time. Then, drum roll; out along the path we went, turning right, through the Pine Trees, turning left down the road a little bit. OMG! We were on our way, all by ourselves. We're doing it!!! It almost feels surreal. Maybe I should pinch myself?

We had an awesome walk down to the front gate; Woody again did not miss a beat. He guided me all the way, so diligent and happy.

Ha ha, I must tell you, my smile hasn't move off my face! I am a tad proud of my beautiful Guide Dog Woody.

We then came home and waited for Danni to arrive. Then it was off to the paddock to catch Lola. Well, guess what happened this morning! I asked Woody to sit outside the gate and stay. I found my way to the gate, called Lola, and gave her a carrot or two, and proceeded to put the halter on. I opened the gate, positioned Lola at the gate and called Woody who came in by my side. Then I said to Woody, "to the tack shed." And off we went. Woody, Lola, and I, to the tack shed.

This felt amazing catching my horse and Woody guiding us up to the tack shed. Once again Woody did this with ease. I took Lola's rug off and gave her a brush. Then Danni led Lola out to the arena. I led the way of course with wonderful Woody. Our destination was the mounting block. Mr Perfect went straight to the mounting block. Wow, just such a good boy.

Everything we do now seems so fluid and easy for him. Woody has not missed a beat over the past four days of training!

We then did some work in the dressage arena, leading Lola around in there. I love it. We did lots of stops, sit, wait for a while, up, stand, walk on. It felt quite amazing; Woody and Lola are walking together as if they have been doing it forever. It's not just my amazing Guide Dog, Lola is just so accepting of what is happening. I am so very blessed to have these two incredible animals in my life.

Then it was back to the tack shed to put Lola's rug on and return her to her paddock. I led Woody and Lola down, Woody sat outside the gate and stayed while I walked Lola into her paddock, let her go, gave her a carrot, shut the gate, called Woody and then we went back to the tack shed.

Then it was time for Woody to have some fun. Our plan was to go out and play with Woody in the dressage arena with one of his toys. He has this lovely big rope toy. Danni went and got it off the veranda and carried it, hiding it from Woody, so he wasn't distracted from his work.

When we got to the dressage arena, I took Woody's harness off. His toy was probably about four meters away sitting on a chair. Even though I thought he wouldn't understand what I was saying, I couldn't resist trying it, I said "find your toy Woody, find your toy." Guess what he did?

He raced straight over to the chair, picked up his toy and walked back to me. Oh, my heavens Woody is next level awesome! Once I got the toy from him, I let him go, got him to sit and stay then I threw his toy as far as I could and let him go. He had so much fun running free in the dressage arena, skylarking, and playing with his rope.

Then it was time for the wonderful Danni to head back to Sydney. It was time for Woody and I to have the next week of training to ourselves. We had lots of things Danni has taught us to work on, lots of homework. But I was so excited. It was going to be a fantastic week. I just knew it.

DAY 6 – OOPS!
CONSISTENCY IS CRITICAL

Take the Time it Takes

Solo for a week. No pressure!
We were off to a great start, I quietly put Woody's harness on and our destination for the day was the dressage arena and the mounting block. Once we got there, I thought I'd take his harness off so he could have a play. In his usual fashion Woody went straight out to the dressage arena, straight to the mounting block.

Oh, my heavens his destination work is so good. I then got his rope toy and played with him for about 20 minutes. Him running and playing. He hasn't quite got the gist of bringing the toy back to me so off we'd go having to look for it. Well, he looks and sniffs, I follow trying to find it with my feet. Yes, I'll have to get it so he brings it back and puts it in my hand, but that will take a little time.

Then it was time to down toys, put his harness on, and head back to the house. But oops, this is where I messed up! I didn't give Woody the right target word, "tack shed." I said, "go home to the house," which wasn't one of our target words. So, because of my inconsistency, I messed up. But we fixed it very quickly and got back on track and came inside.

This worried me because it may have confused Woody. So, I needed to remedy it. So, at lunchtime I asked Matthew would he observe Woody and I going out to the dressage arena, which once again he did perfectly. But this time coming back in I gave Woody the right target which was 'Tack Shed' and it was seamless, he was amazing.

It was also so cool having Matthew there just in case I stuffed up again. But Matthew said Woody was amazing, he missed limbs in trees that I could've hit my head on and went around small trees that could've been an issue. Matthew said he did an extremely good job. Then we came back to the tack shed, then lots of praise and back to the house, up the steps and onto his bed and I took his harness off. He truly is such a good boy.

It is really quite amazing every time I think of him like when I think of Lola the smile comes up from deep inside of me and just beams. I am so blessed to have two amazing animals, both which give me independence and my mobility. This totally rocks.

I would love to describe to you what I'm doing at the moment. I am quietly sitting out on the front veranda I have a glass of wine, my wonderful Woody at my feet, resting his head on my feet, listening to the birds in the garden.

There is a slight breeze, the little Blue Wrens and Parrots are chirping away in the garden. It has been a spectacular day, nearly an autumn type day really. I can hear Lola in her paddock stomping the flies away, and finishing the end of her hay. I can hear the Kookaburras in the distance talking to each other and heralding in the end of the day. The Cockatoos and the Corellas are busy in the trees on the river squawking and talking, getting ready for resting as night draws closer.

It is peaceful, it is blissful. I have one of my best mates sitting at my feet content and happy. I think Thunder Paws the pussycat isn't too far away because I can hear him every now and again purring.

This picture I have painted, I have painted with words. I hope you can feel the breeze and get the chance to listen to the birds. I would love to describe the sunset to you, but I can't do that. But I can tell you it is a magnificent evening, and all is well.

So, tomorrow is another day full of adventures. Tomorrow Woody and I might take Lola for a walk, and maybe Matthew will be able to observe.

As beautiful Johno used to say, "this is a one step at a time gig," and look what we have accomplished in just four days of training!

P.S. Matthew reminded me that when it is dark for me, it's not for everybody else.

DAY 7 – A LITTLE APPREHENSIVE

So grateful   ©Guide Dogs NSW

Wow! Just a little apprehensive!

Once again, the day is off to a wonderful start. It is a spectacular morning again, a little autumn like. A little bit of a cool breeze, but very pleasant to be out working with my beautiful Woody. I had a few things to do today other than feeding my beautiful Lola, and the Kookaburras and taking Woody for his morning walk. I also had a couple of domestic goddess duties to get around today. One of which was the washing. I will get back to this in a minute.

I had plans today of possibly taking Lola and Woody to the dressage arena, but Matthew was very busy today and really didn't have time. He did though make time to put a post in to tie Woody up at his kennel at the dressage arena, which was wonderful. Woody should be very happy at the dressage arena; his kennel is very flash, and it has loads of shade.

But I was feeling a little apprehensive this morning probably because I stuffed up yesterday with the training and I didn't want to do that again. So, we did some more target work going out to the dressage arena using the mounting block as the target. Woody did this effortlessly. We sat out there having some quality time sitting together, him getting used to being patient. Which I have to admit is something I'm not very good at. So, it was probably good for both of us, and it was beautiful out in the sunshine just sitting with my mate Woody.

Coming back in from the dressage arena I used the target word "tack shed." Woohoo Mother Magoo! He rocked! No deviation, no curve in the line, bam! Straight to the tack shed.

Matthew then joined us for a little while so we thought we would teach Woody a new destination. What about something that helps me when I take the washing out to the clothesline to hang it up, and go get it once its dry? I have to get the washing basket from the house into the trolley out at the clothesline. So, Woody and I did a practise run without the clothes basket, using Matthew as the target for the clothesline. Straight to Matthew and the clothesline. Good boy! Lots of praise and loads of treats!

Then I targeted him going back to the house, I said, "and in we go." Woody stopped at the veranda stairs, took me up the stairs one at a time, then sat on his mat. I asked him to sit and stay and I went in and got the clothes basket. Now this next bit was going to be very interesting – I had a loaded wash basket in one hand and Woody's harness in the other. I was a bit worried about going down the steps, but I shouldn't have been. We did that with ease.

I then put the clothes in the clothes basket trolley, and I asked Woody to walk on and he led me. I pulled the trolley with the clothes in it and said, "out to the clothesline." He went straight to Matthew and the clothesline, what a good boy, again loads of praise and a wee treat. I then asked him to sit by the washing basket while I hung the clothes out. He did not move; he is just so happy to be with me and doing things with me. I can't believe the bond we have already in such a short time. I am so grateful.

So, okay we didn't get to do any Lola work today, just going down to her gate and back, but that is okay. Everything worked beautifully and neither Woody nor I were taken out of our comfort zone. But we did learn a new destination, go Woody!

I would like to take the opportunity to thank Guide Dogs Australia for the most amazing, wonderful Guide Dog Woody. He has brought to my life independence, mobility, and a freedom which I have never had on the farm. It is incredible how I feel now about my backyard, my home. I so appreciate it.

A massive shout out to whoever the amazing person was who trained Woody. He has been trained so well. He is an exceptional Guide Dog. I have had six other Guide Dogs to measure him by, he is outstanding.

I would also like to thank the wonderful people who puppy walked Woody. You all did such a wonderful job, he is such a magnificent dog because of how he was trained when he was a baby. I am so grateful to everybody who has had a hand in Woody being with me, being my Guide Dog. Thank you from the bottom of my heart.

I don't know whether you ever think about walking in someone else's shoes or not, but how about right now you give it a whirl. Close your eyes and stick your feet in my shoes for just a little while. It's dark, it can get scary, I can get lost in the bedroom! Yes, I am like a ping-pong ball going up the hallway from one side to the other. Then I walk outside, and there he is, my beautiful Guide Dog sitting on his bed. He sits, I put his harness on and quietly ask him to stand up. He guides me straight to the steps. We go down them one step at a time. He guides me directly to the tack shed with confidence, in a straight line. He sits, I give him a pat and thank him, sometimes I give him a treat. Then I will grab a carrot from in the tack shed and ask Woody to stand up, let's find Lola, and he quietly turns around and walks straight down to Lola's paddock.

I have NEVER walked straight down to Lola's paddock in my life! Why? Because I haven't had someone guiding me other than if I have someone's arm. I do now, and that is the beautiful Woody who has given me the independence and freedom to be confident and to walk down to Lola's paddock, just like you would walk to your horse's paddock. I now have my best mate beside me, guiding me.

This beautiful Guide Dog Woody has given me a newfound independence of freedom. I can't explain to you how amazingly grateful I am for this. Most people take walking from A to B for granted. The fact that you can just get up and walk to your stables or walk and catch your horse, walk out to your garden and not get lost or ouched is wonderful. Like you, I can do that now. With the help of my beautiful Guide Dog. I love my life. Thank you Woody.

The independence and mobility Woody brings to my life on the farm is mind blowing. With my other Guide Dogs, in particular my wonderful Guide Dog Eccles, I was able to travel the world. I competed in Atlanta at the Paralympics, Denmark at the World Championships, New Zealand at the Trans-Tasman Dressage Competition, all because of my beautiful Guide Dogs.

I have been blessed with being able to have the independence and mobility to do whatever I would like to do, thank you beautiful four-legged animals. My beautiful horse does the same thing, she brings that amazing independence and mobility. When I ride, you don't know I'm blind.

So, needless to say, I'm excited to see where the wonderful Woody, Lola and I go in the future. But again, nothing happens without beautiful friends to make my dreams come true.

DAY 8 – DREAMS DO COME TRUE

Working Together

What a cracker of a training session I had working with Woody and Lola today!

It's been another beautiful day here on the Macquarie River, another beautiful autumn type day. We've had a slight breeze and it's been a little coolish, but it's been pleasant.

Okay, day eight of Woody and I working together, we are now totally solo. I have my wonderful friend Gwen coming out to observe and make sure everything is safe. But how clever is this amazing Guide Dog. Each morning, and a couple of times during the day without a harness on, Woody takes me to the porch steps, he quietly goes down the steps without a harness on, I give him the command "to the loo," and he takes me out through the Pine Trees, out into the garden where I toilet him.

I get him to sit, I put him on a long lead, and he goes quick. This is all done without the harness on. When he has finished, he comes back and sits beside me. I shorten the lead and say "inside Woody, inside" and off he goes, guiding me back through the Pine Trees to the house. He stops at the bottom of the steps, waits for me to signal him to walk on then takes them one step at a time. Right up until he guides me to his bed on the porch, is all done WITHOUT HIS HARNESS on! He is perfect.

So, this morning I have butterflies in my stomach. My plan is a bold one. Today Woody and I are going out to the tack shed to get Lola some carrots and wait for Gwen. I now carry two bum bags; one with Lola treats, one with Woody treats. How hilarious.

When Gwen arrived I asked her not to make a fuss of Woody or even make eye contact with him. She is to wait till he gets used to her. Oh he was really good. He went to stand once, I asked him to "sit down, stay, good boy Woody." I then explained to Gwen what our plan for the day was, she was going to observe and take photos and if she thought I was in trouble she could talk to me and let me know what was happening.

So here goes, this is how that plan went. This is what happened.

From the tack shed I said, "find Lola, find Lola Woody." And he guided me to Lola's paddock. Lola saw us coming and met us at the gate. I asked Woody to "sit and stay." I opened the gate; Gwen handed me Lola's halter; I gave her a carrot. I put her halter on, opened the gate, and then called Woody to my side. We stood for a minute, had a breather, then I asked Woody to take me to the tack shed, "to the tack shed Woody, to the tack shed." Off we went, and he took me straight to the tack shed, then went and sat beside the drum he sits at.

For safety I tie Woody to the drum. He sat and stayed while Gwen and I took Lola's rugs off and gave her a brush. We put her bell boots on and were ready to go. I unhooked Woody's lead from the drum, quietly took Lola's lead and said to Woody, "to the dressage arena Woody, to the dressage arena," and we were off. Woody guiding me confidently out to the dressage arena. As we were getting closer, I said, "to the mounting block Woody, to the mounting block," and he guides Lola and I to the mounting block with such confidence ease.

Today was a big experiment. Woody has never seen Lola trot or canter, so I thought I would tie him at his kennel at the dressage arena and then lunge Lola so he could observe the horse doing something other than quietly standing in the paddock.

It was wonderful having Gwen there as she could tell me if Woody was standing or being distracted. He only stood two times and Gwen just went over to him and asked him to sit, down, and stay. This was so cool. I am so grateful for Gwen's help. Woody took no notice of me lunging Lola in the walk, trot or canter. This was a win-win for all of us. I'm so pleased.

I then brought Lola out of the dressage arena and went and put Woody's harness back on while Gwen held Lola for me. Woody then led me back over to Lola, and I said to Woody "to the tack shed Woody, to the tack shed," and once again, with such confidence and ease, Woody guided me back to the tack shed. By this stage I am nearly busting at the seams with excitement.

This is what I have dreamt about, being independent and able to do all of this with my horse, myself. And not only by myself, but regardless of whether it is overcast or not. Typically, I orientate myself by feeling the suns warmth on my face. I know I'm going in a particular direction if the sun is warming my right check versus if it warming my left cheek, or the front of my face. When the sun plays hide and seek and goes behind the clouds, I lose my orientation. This can be frustrating, scary and so not fun.

I don't have to worry what game the sun is playing now. Woody can orientate me. Lucky me!

Woody goes straight to his drum and sits down. I tie him to the drum, and Lola to her tie up point. Woody sits and stays while I go into the tack shed and get Lola a clean rug. We give her a brush, take her bell boots off and rug her. We are now ready for the last part of our days' work; Woody leading Lola and I back down to Lola's paddock. Which I must say he has down pat. He is a total legend, straight down to her paddock we go, I ask him to "sit Woody, stay Woody." I walk through the gate, let Lola go, shut the gate, and then called Woody to my side. When he arrives, I give him a big pat and a treat. What an amazing Guide Dog you are Woody.

This is only day eight of Woody and I working together. WOW! I am totally blown away with this amazing Guide Dogs initiative and work ethic. I cannot wipe the smile off my face. I am so very grateful to have this beautiful Guide Dog in my life. And here was I thinking I would never get another Guide Dog. Wow haven't things changed.

Beautiful Woody is now sitting on the veranda with a bone, having a chew and relaxing. I have come back inside for more domestic goddess duties. I'm hopeful tomorrow we can replicate what we did today.

Eventually I would like Woody to be able to take us out to the dressage arena and I ride Lola. But I will introduce that slowly, I don't want Woody to get frightened about my interaction with Lola. Hence why it was important for him to start seeing how fast and slow Lola goes, how I can lunge her. This is all important stuff for him to become aware of what happens with the horse and my interaction with the horse.

But if today is any indication, Woody is going to take no notice when I ride Lola.

DAY 9 – MEANT TO BE

Building Trust, Confidence & Love

Somethings are just meant to be.

Wow another beautiful morning, lovely cool breeze, spectacular sunshine. What more could you ask for.

Well once again my Guide Dog Woody is shining like an evening star. This morning he totally rocked with all his destination work; going to the tack shed, going down to get Lola. I thought we were going to have to teach him a new destination "find Lola" but Lola decided to come up to us. I would still like to introduce that command in the next few days, getting Woody to find Lola. That'll be a handy destination. He has already started finding Matthew for me, which is very cool.

So, I put the head stall on Lola and Woody led us back up to the tack shed. Gwen and I took her rug off and gave her a big brush, put her bell boots on to be worked. Okay I get it; this is all starting to sound a little monotonous, but this amazing Guide Dog is totally knocking it out of the ballpark.

Most Guide Dogs aren't this far advanced in just nine days training. And don't forget our Guide Dog trainer Danni left after four days training. I am blown away by this dog's initiative. He wants so much to please. Keeping in mind I have had six other Guide Dogs to compare him to, Woody is totally exceptional.

After Lola had been brushed, I took up Woody's harness and asked him to take Lola and I out to the dressage arena. When we got a little closer to the dressage arena, I used our target which is the mounting block. He took me straight to the mounting block, I gave him a big pat and a lot of praise, such a good boy. Gwen held Lola while I put Woody in his kennel which he loves. I then put the lunge lead on Lola, and we walked out to the arena and today I did more like what I would normally do, 15 minutes each side lunging. Woody was such a good boy. Only once did Gwen have to ask him to sit and down.

After I had finished working Lola, Woody guided Lola, and I back to the tack shed. She got another big brush, put a clean rug on and then back to her paddock.

Woody is just totally amazing. I keep thinking about the day Danni told me about when she drove past our driveway and pulled up another driveway to turn around, as soon as she started driving down our driveway that Woody stood up. The only time he stood up the whole trip from Sydney.

Oh my heavens, having Woody in my life was just meant to be. Woody knew where he was coming to, and it is as if he has lived here all his life. He has just fitted in to farm life amazingly well. Even Thunder Paws our cat is accepting him. And if you knew Thunder Paws you would realise, he accepts nobody. But Woody has won him over.

So, tomorrow's goal will be doing virtually the same as we did today, but I will saddle Lola up and work her in her saddle and then have a ride. I'll introduce this slowly, so Woody doesn't get upset about me interacting with Lola and being on her back. I think it is so important to introduce these things slowly and not have hick ups and misunderstandings. So really looking forward to our session tomorrow. And what about our beautiful Lola, she also has not missed a beat. With Woody guiding us around she has just taken it one step at a time, no fuss, and she thinks it's really cool that I have two bum bags with treats in them, one for Lola and one for Woody.

Also thought I had to share this with you. Matthew often takes Woody out to toilet him of an evening, not in harness, just with the lead on and Woody stops at the top of the steps for Matthew, goes down the steps one at a time, and when Matthew brings him back in, he stops at the bottom of the steps and goes up one at a time. Woody is doing everything with Matthew that he does with me, how cool is my dog.

DAY 10 – WE'VE GOT THIS

Trust

This is what dreams are made of.

Another spectacular day, just a tad warmer today I think probably a little over 30°. We were off to an awesome start this morning. Woody guided us down and caught Lola, we went to the tack shed and saddled up, all before Gwen arrived. This was a huge accomplishment. All by ourselves we did it all. I am so proud of Woody and Lola; it was so cool.

When Gwen arrived, she finished putting on Lola's bell boots while I put her bridle on. Then we headed out to the dressage arena. Once again Woody was on fire. He worked perfectly, taking us straight to the mounting block. Gwen held Lola while I put Woody at his kennel. I will have to spray around his kennel this afternoon for ants, as he couldn't stay sitting on the sand. The ants would have bit him. Hence, he stayed inside his lovely big kennel.

I then took Lola into the dressage arena and gave her a little bit of a lunge. She was such a good girl, super-duper transitions, two or three strides of canter, then two or three strides of trot and then back to the canter. Her transitions were really sharp.

When we finished Gwen brought the mounting block out for me and took all the lunging gear off and hung it up. Woody was taking no notice of any of the proceedings happening in the arena, he was busy chewing on his bone. Then I mounted Lola and got Gwen just to let me know if Woody seemed distressed or upset. Well, you probably guessed it, he took no notice. So off I went.

I rode around the arena, a couple of changes of direction with a nice long relaxed rein. Lola was stepping out beautifully, but for me a critical thing was ensuring that Woody was happy.

If he was taking no notice of us riding at a walk, let's try the trot. So, I did a little bit of trotting, lots of transitions back to the walk and back to the trot again at the end of the arena that was closest to Woody, near the kennel. Guess what he did?

Yes, again he took no notice. So I quietly asked Lola to go into the canter, we did lots of circles and transitions and diagonals. Woody still took no notice. I was riding my horse with my Guide Dog happy near us, does it get any better!

Oh my heavens what an amazing day this is for me. This is what dreams are made of. Okay, at the moment I'm not out competing, that will come. But what a milestone, my Guide Dog led my horse and I out to the arena and I am now riding my horse and my Guide Dog is sitting quietly. This totally rocks.

After I finished riding, Woody led Lola and I back to the tack shed. We unsaddled Lola, and Gwen and I gave Lola a lovely bath. Once again Woody just sat and watched, he didn't try to participate, he just sat and watched and was Mr Perfect.

I did some carrot exercises with Lola, then put her rug on and Woody led Lola and I down to her paddock. Woody sits and lies down just outside Lola's paddock, I tell him to stay, and I walked the next couple of strides into Lola's paddock, shut the gate and let her go and gave her a biscuit of hay.

Oh what a cracker of a morning. The smile hasn't moved off my face. When I'm working with Woody and Lola the smile very rarely moves off my face. I am so grateful for what these two beautiful animals bring to my life, the love, the happiness, the joy, the independence, the freedom. This is what dreams are made of for me.

My goal is to be able to do all of this without someone with me. For now, it is wonderful having Gwen here to keep an eye on things, to let me know if somethings not working right, or if Woody is standing when he is meant to be lying down. It's good to have those eyes on the ground.

I am so looking forward to tomorrow and doing a few more destinations with Woody. We might even get to walk down to the front gate tomorrow morning early, let's see how we go. And then I'll work Lola again, I can't wait. She is such a good girl and so relaxed now, it is amazing just giving her time to realise she doesn't have to rush, she can relax and enjoy being ridden, instead of being so wound up and tense all the time.

DAY 11 – GOING SOLO

The 3 Musketeers

Wow, wow, and wow. We did it!

Okey-dokey, today was our first day totally solo. Woody, Lola, and I, we were off to a good start. I filled up Lola's bum bag with carrots, and Woody's bum bag with dog treats. I went out and put Woody's harness on and we went down the stairs, straight to the tack shed. I got all the things I would need to saddle up Lola like the saddle, the saddle cloth, girth, bridle, work boots and so on, and had them sitting outside on the saddle stand. Then I got Woody and I said, "to Lola's paddock."

Woody guided me down to Lola perfectly. He sat outside Lola's paddock, and I called Lola. She came for a carrot of course, she took a little bit of coaxing, but she did it. I called Woody to the gate and gave him the command, "to the tack shed." He took us straight up to the tack shed. I tied Lola up, then tied Woody up, took her rugs off and gave her a big brush. All the time Woody just sitting quietly. I'm assuming he was watching us, or he was probably snoring.

Once Lola was tacked up I untied Woody and we were off to the dressage arena. Straight out to the mounting block, and then I said, "to your kennel Woody." He went straight to his kennel, I took his harness off, tied him up and gave him his bone so he had something to do while I was riding. All the time I was thinking "oh my heavens, we are doing this, we are doing it all by ourselves and it is totally awesome." I gave Lola a quiet lunge, walk, trot, and canter both ways, and then we came out of the dressage arena lined up on the mounting block and off I went riding my beautiful Lola.

By this time, I have to tell you, my cup was running over with joy. I was so, so happy and so excited.

This is what you dream of doing, being able to do all of these beautiful things by yourself. I do them with my beautiful Guide Dog guiding me up with my lovely horse. I get on my horse and ride her while Woody sits in his kennel and watches. Oh my heavens I am so, so ecstatically happy. Beautiful Woody and Lola, thank you for the happiness, the joy, the love, the independence, the mobility, and freedom you bring to my life. I am so grateful, and so excited.

But I have to tell you, I really wasn't quite alone. I often talk of guardian angels, and I have two beautiful guardian angels living next door. My wonderful mother and father-in-law Lee and John. They both watched me this morning having Woody guide me out to the arena leading Lola. They watched me while I rode Lola. They watched us come back in, and then they sent me a beautiful message of how lovely it was to see us being so independent. It made me cry, well it also made me cry when Lola, Woody and I got back to the tack shed. Tears of joy, oh my heavens this is wonderful.

To my beautiful guardian angels in the house next door, thank you. I am so grateful for your love and your support and always being there for me. I love you both.

DAY 12 – WHAT A DIFFERENCE 14 DAYS MAKE

He's a Keeper!   © Guide Dogs NSW

What a difference two weeks makes.

Less than two weeks ago I was still getting zapped on the electric fence with my white cane. I was walking into the arms of the prickly lemon tree and getting caught up in low tree branches. I was still getting lost in the garden!

Now look at us less than two weeks later.

Who could have imagined in less than two weeks, I am moving around the garden with such freedom, confidence, and a smile that won't leave. I no longer worry that I'm going to bitten by the electric fence or get lost in the garden.

All because of a wonderful Guide Dog Woody.

When I reflect on it, I know how hard it was using my white cane to get from point A to point B. With Lola it was important that when I did this, I had someone who could keep an eye on me and make sure I was safe, I kept getting lost!

We often take things for granted.

Oh my heavens, I am, well not quite, speechless, because I'm still talking, but I am so excited about what Woody has brought to my life. This newfound independence on the farm and all of the amazing things I can do with my Guide Dog and my horse and do it independently. I can do it confidently. I wish there was a word that could explain how this feels. My life has a shine and a sparkle to it now. Woody has brought magic to my life. My life is now totally awesome.

Okay enough of my excitedness. Today Janelle and Jacqueline were coming, my coaches. Nell was going to ride Lola for me. But first we had a big job to do. We had to fix the arena!

The arena is a 60m x 20m flat space that is filled with sand. Around the outside of that space is a small white edge, made of plastic. Think a very very low fence, less than knee height. We had a seriously huge storm, and all those edge pieces were blown around. So, Matthew and I started putting it all back up. While Nell caught Lola and tacked her up, Jacq helped Matt and I. Oh, my heavens many hands make light work. Generally, it takes me at least two, maybe two and a half hours to put the arena back up with Matthew. With the extra help it was done in no time at all.

While Nell was warming Lola up in the arena, I went back to the house to harness up Woody. We kept up our target work, we went to the "tack shed." He sat and I gave him lots of praise. Then I said, "to the dressage arena Woody, to the dressage arena." Straight out to the Dressage arena he went. As we got closer to the mounting block I said, "to the mounting block Woody, to the mounting block." Straight to the mounting block he went. After a big pat I said, "to your kennel Woody," and he went and sat outside his kennel. I took his harness off and put it on the kennel and I found myself a seat beside the kennel. To help keep him occupied I gave him a bone to chew on. He's happily in the kennel, not moving.

I am so grateful to Jacqueline who acts as my eyes when Nell is giving Lola a lesson. She tells me what's going on. Nell asked for and got lots of beautiful leg yields, keeping Lola parallel to the long side. I could hear how lovely their rhythm and regularity. It was a super-duper ride.

They then did lots of transitions; canter through to trot, back to the walk, into the trot, into the canter and then setting Lola up, getting her to slow the canter, sit tall, breathe out, and walk. Nell is such a lovely soft rider, they nailed this exercise, it was lovely to hear.

They also did some work on doing canter pirouettes. In the canter, not too tight, just nice big ones. Lola on the circle, with Nell inviting Lola's hindquarters in, asking her to slow a little, sit, half halt with the outside rein, half halt with the outside rein, outside leg guiding her round, softness to the inside. Woohoo! Nell nailed it. Absolutely wonderful. I wish I could've seen Nell's face. She would have been smiling.

Nell rode Lola back to the tack shed with Woody and I following. Woody sat at the tack shed while we took Lola's saddle and bridle off. He did not move, he was not interested in meeting Nell and Jacq, he sat quietly. Such a good boy. I am so very proud of him.

When the girls left and Lola had been put in her paddock and given some liquorice, I came inside to do domestic goddess duties. You know the washing, the ironing and all that stuff. But I'm still smiling at how it felt with my new independence, listening to Lola's happy rhythmical foot falls in the sand was music to my ears.

DAY 13 – WOW WHAT A DAY!

Happy Days

Learning another destination.
I was up extra early this morning as Lola, and I were having an early lesson. Hence, she had to be fed very early as I like her to have had her feed at least two hours before she's ridden. She had a lovely big biscuit of hay. Having that bit of time after her feed all helps with her gut health.

I am so grateful for Woody. I grab my white cane; it is dark outside, so I have no sun to rely on for my orientation. I tap out the path, I'm doing okay heading towards the tack shed to get Lola's feed. But this is where things go pair shaped. I end up running into one of the pine tree limbs. I have no idea where it is. I can't yell out for Matthew as I will wake Matthew's mum and dad and scare the hell out of them next door. So I spent 10 minutes wandering around the garden this morning, trying to reorientate myself. I was lost! It was frightening.

I kept tapping around until I found something familiar, a tub with a plant in it beside a chair near the tack shed. Oh, my heavens, it felt so good to find something familiar. My heart was racing, and I so didn't want to call out for help.

So, eventually I got to the tack shed door to organise Lola's feed and headed down to her gate. Again, this was tedious and time-consuming as there was no sun to orientate myself with its warmth on my face. So, I headed off along the rosemary bushes and then headed for the arms of the Lemon Tree with its prickles, and then tapped my way to Lola's gate where she met me waiting for her feed.

So, I fed our beautiful Lola and stood in the dark with her giving her a pat for a little while, and then headed back to the tack shed. Then I came in and took Woody out to the toilet, swearing I will never do a trip in the dark again without Woody by my side guiding me. It really was such a scary experience and I thought I was over that. I really should've known better, and I should've used Woody this morning.

But with all stories there is a silver lining. After I had my breakfast, I went out and organised the saddle, bridle, saddle cloth, work boots and so on. I got everything set up and went to get Lola ready for our lesson.

I headed off with my pocket full of carrots for her and treats for Woody in my bum bag. As per usual Woody is magnificent, straight down to Lola's paddock via the stand where I keep her halter. Woody sits and waits. Still no Lola. She is not coming today, so I stand and contemplate, do we have to teach Woody a new destination – "find Lola."

So, this is how things played out.

Lola did not appear so Woody, and I went into her paddock, I just keep saying, "find Lola Woody, find Lola." Well, he wanders across the top of the paddock and often Lola is just the other side of her water trough, it seemed this was the direction we were heading. God love his cotton socks, Woody guides me straight to Lola. I got him to sit, I put the halter on her, gave her a treat then said to Woody, "to the gate and back to the tack shed."

Oh, my heavens! This amazing Guide Dog did not miss a beat. He guided me along the top of the paddock, he stopped while I found the step out of her paddock, there is quite a large rise, I didn't want to trip, then he headed off guiding me to the tack shed.

I hooked Lola up first and then I tied Woody to his drum and gave him a treat for being such an amazing boy and learning a new destination – "find Lola." Everything from there went swimmingly. I gave Lola a big brush, saddled her up, then Woody guided us to the arena and off he went straight to his kennel. There he sat down; I took his harness off and inside he went out of the crisp wind. What a good boy.

My lesson today with Lola was awesome, we worked on accuracy, remembering that accuracy is the thing that gives us our points in the lower levels and it's important in the higher levels too. We worked on doing a transition, if you were going to do an extended trot from K across to M, you collect in the corner, after you shorten the stride you gather the energy, you turn at K, put the letter M between the horse's ears and then you squeeze and get the horse to do an extended trot, not a run but an extended trot.

Then we worked on a couple of exercises doing three loops called Serpentines, Lola has this going so well, also getting that perfect 20-meter circle, remembering there are no straight lines on a circle. Today was another awesome lesson. I am totally loving the transition work and our accuracy.

I will be doing the hard yards during the week, doing more training and playing with our beautiful Lola, and having Woody guiding us from point A to B.

Thank heavens for no more getting lost in the garden with my white cane.

DAY 14 – RIVER WALK

It's just 'A Walk in the Park'

Spectacular morning

What an amazing time of the year! The mornings are quite brisk, and a wee breeze blows early. I am generally up at about 6.30am each morning feeding Lola. The mornings are spectacular.

You know it's the things that cost nothing that I would like to see; a sunset, a sunrise, the little birds in the garden, the smile on Woody's face when we are working, my beautiful horse Lola, my handsome husband Matthew. The things in life that cost nothing, things probably we take for granted. But that's a dream.

While on my way down to feed beautiful Lola, I am greeted with a whinny. I gave her a pat and a carrot and her breakfast. Then back to toilet wonderful Woody. I now take him out and he guides me out through the garden without the harness on and I unclick his lead and he does his toileting without the lead on. He then has a bit of a run around and comes back when I call him. Thank heavens he's such a good boy.

Today I'm waiting for the wonderful Guide Dog trainer Danni to come and see how we've been going. We're going into Dubbo to do a walk along the Macquarie River. There are lovely walking tracks around Dubbo, so we are going to do a bit of this for training for our pending hundred kilometre challenge. This is a fundraiser for the Western Cancer Council foundation. The money we raise will go into research at the local hospital, which is all very exciting.

It was a beautiful morning for a walk.

We came across a lovely lady pushing her pram with a couple of dogs and Woody just stopped and sat and watched them go past. What a good boy. He wasn't distracted by the other dogs. This is important as you could realise that other dogs can be a big distraction, and it is so appreciated when people have their dogs on the lead and under control.

We also stopped and talked to a couple of people. One of them asked if they may pat Woody, and I said no sorry you can't pat my Guide Dog when he is working. When a Guide Dog has their harness on it is important that their work is not interrupted. Patting him would interrupt his work. You also can't feed a Guide Dog in harness; they need to be focused on their handler. They were very understanding with my explanation, but not all people do understand the important job a Guide Dog has, or how important it is not to interrupt them when they are working.

With my other Guide Dogs, I have had problems with other dogs attacking them when they are walking through town, or people calling out to the dog or whistling to the dog. This is such a no, no, and so disappointing when people do this because it just drops the dog's concentration. These aren't just a dog with some harness on. They are responsible for my life! Today was a good day for going for a walk, but it was also wonderful that we were able to educate another couple of people about Guide Dog etiquette.

I had a great question from a man named Mitch. He asked why I tie Woody up when I come back to the tack shed to work with Lola. It is mainly at this stage because Woody is learning the ropes. It could be a safety issue. If I tie Woody up, I know where he is. Keeping in mind I am totally blind so I cannot see if he comes over or is too close to Lola.

At this stage I am keeping Lola and Woody a good four feet apart. When Woody is sitting near his drum, he is safe, and Lola has her side of the rail to stand on. I can brush and look after her there, knowing she is also safe. But eventually I won't need to tie him up, he'll sits and stay where he's told to. But while we are learning, we just keep it all very safe, I don't want him to have a fright. He is such an exceptional Guide Dog.

Hence starting with introducing Lola to him by going down and feeding her Lola carrots. This way it was done slowly. Then we introduced Danni leading Lola, and then we went out to the dressage arena, Woody at his kennel, and I lunging Lola. Then Woody started leading Lola and I around the dressage arena.

The importance of one step at a time for Woody is equally important when working with horses. It is important not to over face the Guide Dog. I don't want either Woody or Lola to get a fright. So as our beautiful Johno used to say, one step at a time. And as a team, oh my heavens, Lola, Woody, and the Blind Chick are rocking out! It is too cool, and I am so proud of both my beautiful animals.

After our lovely walk this morning we went to our favourite cafe Alchemy for morning tea. Danni and I had our usual smashed avocado. We were joined by my wonderful mother and father-in-law Lee and John. It was such a lovely morning. Woody was amazing at the Alchemy Café; he just sat in the corner. The wonderful girls bring him out a drink of water and he sits and has a rest while we enjoyed a lovely meal and great company.

So, onto another training session tomorrow. We will probably go and visit our friend Deb at Marsh Carney Saddlery in Dubbo. This is one of my usual shops for buying horse gear. It will be very cool having Woody take me shopping. I am looking forward to the experience.

DAY 15 – MAGIC DOES HAPPEN

Best Mates   ©MegRose Photography

Well, it's a certain kind of Magic.
I have been sitting thinking about what to write today and it's all about magic, choices and moving forward. I was trying to think when magic first ended in my life. But on reflection, I think it has been there all the time. My life has been blessed with wonderful adventures, mainly with my horses and my Guide Dogs. They have allowed me to travel the world, go on adventures, experience new things, and give me the confidence to have a go.

I think having magic in your life is pretty cool. We create our own magic, and we have the ability to bring more magic and beautiful things into our lives because of our attitude and our choices.

This has all come up because I said something about my beautiful Guide Dog Woody, and the magic he has brought to my life, as well as the freedom and the independence.

I was asked, "what's the difference between Woody and your other Guide Dogs?" I have been giving this a lot of thought. Really and truly, I have had a couple of years to reflect on not having a Guide Dog. This happened because the NDIS offered me amazing independence and mobility by having the ability to pay someone to take me shopping, doing errands and helping me with things. But guess what, they can't be here all the time. Hence, I spent most of the time on the farm by myself with my white cane.

Keeping in mind I have never used my Guide Dogs on the farm and my sense of orientation has gotten so bad, I have no idea where I am at any time. I use the sun for my orientation. This is why I am so much better at orientating myself of a morning than I am of an evening, the sun is where I walk and when I'm going down to Lola it shines on the right-hand side of my face. I feed Lola and I come back, and it shines on the left-hand side of my face. So, I know I am heading south because the sun is in the east. You know that this is total magic, just being able to use our beautiful sunshine to help me with my orientation.

But I digress. In the years of not having a Guide Dog, I have spent a lot of time getting lost in the garden. Johno used to share a lot of the stories about me getting lost in his paddock, getting hit by the electric fence with my white cane, and yes, who could forget the dreaded lemon tree with its prickles. Then enter stage left, 15 days ago an amazing Guide Dog called Woody.

He has a certain magic about him. I think with my other six Guide Dogs I haven't allowed them to come into my heart because they have been my work dogs, and a work tool. And it is really important that a Guide Dog is used as a Guide Dog, they are not a pet. A lot of time and effort goes into training these magnificent dogs, making them a pet spoils all that training.

But with Woody, I have allowed my heart to open, and I think that's where the magic is. Having that open heart, and that love and willingness to allow something to come into your heart. Yes opening up might break it, but that's okay. It's better to have loved and lost, than never to have loved at all.

So, on reflection I truly think one of the magic things Woody has brought into my life, apart from my independence, my mobility, and freedom, which is just extraordinary, he has also brought a bucket load of love, cuddles, and just being a very cool mate. I think this opening of my heart has only happened because of not having a Guide Dog for so long and realising the importance of the independence and mobility and the love. The magic of love has been a bonus.

It's really interesting my horses have always been in my heart, and I have always been open to the love horses bring to me. But I have not allowed it with my Guide Dogs, which I find really interesting. Except for wonderful Woody.

It's like when I think of our beautiful Johno, and I reflect on the amazing journey we had. Two years and two days with him struggling with Equine Shivers, trying to find a way to give him the best life possible, and the best quality life possible. Every day was full of ups and downs, but always with love compassion and care. Then our beautiful Johno became an angel.

There was such a gap in my life. A hole in my heart. I am not whole without a horse in my life. How lucky was I to find Lola. I am so grateful for the amazing opportunity Jacinta gave me, having Lola on free lease and then Matthew bought her for me. So grateful, and my heart, even though we had lost Johno, my heart needed to have another horse. Lola has filled my heart with so much joy and love and dreams. There goes more of that beautiful magic stuff, that love stuff, that stuff we take for granted sometimes.

I had a wonderful day training with Woody today. We went for another walk along the Macquarie River and did a bit of retail therapy by visiting our beautiful friend Deb at Marsh Carney Saddlery. And then, you guessed it, we went and had a smashed avocado lunch at our favourite cafe Alchemy.

We have a big day planned for our training tomorrow. We are going into Dubbo to do some work in town along the main street, Macquarie Street. Focusing on street crossings and people and businesses. I know I was only going to use Woody on the farm, but I'm sure we will be doing lots and lots of other adventures which will require us going into town, maybe going shopping with our friends. I would also like to look at, a little down the track, maybe doing a couple of local shows with our beautiful Lola and taking her in lead classes. That's another thing to work on, that should be loads of fun.

I guess you have noticed by now that my Guide Dog Woody and I can go virtually everywhere and anywhere legally, cafes, restaurants, shopping, to the butchers, to the bakers. We can go in taxis, cars, aeroplanes, buses, and this is all done legally because he is a Guide Dog. It is illegal to not allow a Guide Dog into your venue. There are only two places they can't go; into a zoo because it is a quarantine area, and into sections of a hospital like intensive care.

But other than that, we can go everywhere.

I have been blessed to have travelled the world with my Guide Dogs. I am looking forward to getting out and about with our beautiful Woody, doing speaking engagements again now that COVID lockdowns are over, and we can get back to living without restrictions.

*

Journal - On reflection

Beautiful Memories   ©Guide Dogs NSW

Wow! Do you ever sit and reflect on your life and how things play out? Do you think about what comes and goes in your life and how it all makes you feel?

I spend quite a bit of time by myself, so I get quite a bit of time to reflect. A lot of my reflection is on how very lucky I am. Okay not so lucky to be totally blind, but lucky in many, many other ways.

Take for instance the independence and mobility I get from riding my beautiful horse! When I put my foot in the stirrup and sit in the saddle, I'm home! I'm where I'm meant to be. I also have the use of two beautiful brown eyes that guide me around the arena and that look after me. With those brown eyes I can accomplish many things. There's exquisite pleasure from being in a trusting partnership, of working together and training together.

I can set goals and reach great heights, but I think there is something incredibly special in the bond that I have with my beautiful horse Lola. The fact that she brings me such independence and freedom. When I'm riding Lola, I look just like everybody else. No one knows I'm blind. Lola makes up for all of that.

Okay I get the pleasure, I have goals and aspirations, and I would love Lola and I to do Dressage competitions. I would love to take her swimming at the beach, and I want to go out mustering. I used to do that as a kid, and I so want all of those beautiful things happening again in my life. Being blind isn't a good enough reason not to be doing it, or not to have a go.

Then enter stage left, a beautiful caramel coloured dog called Woody. He is a Guide Dog and has had many people training him over his two years of life. He has had people walking him when he was a puppy, Puppy Walkers, then he went off to Guide Dog School for training. Now he's with me, the Blind Chick, his handler.

It is hard to explain to you the independence and the sheer feel of freedom and joy I get when I work with Woody. He makes me feel just like everybody else. I can go from one place to the other on the farm without fear of bumping into low hanging branches or getting zapped on an electric fence or falling over something.

I had an amazing conversation with my mother-in-law Lee the other day, she said it is lovely to see me walking out again so freely and confidently. That made my heart sing. Like who would think that two amazing animals can bring such joy, happiness, love, mobility, and freedom to one person.

When Woody and I go walking it's like someone else going walking with their pet except I hold the handle and Woody's two beautiful brown eyes are my eyes, he keeps me safe. He walks me around trees, around puddles, around limbs. I used to get hit in the head by those darn branches, and I used to get lost in the garden all the time. Now we glide through the garden, it's a magical feeling. I wish you could see my face now. It is beaming with a smile every time I think of my new freedom.

I am so very grateful to Guide Dogs NSW for what they have brought to my life over the past 42 years. As you know, Woody is my seventh Guide Dog, and he is totally amazing. But all of my Guide Dogs have brought something special to my life in their own individual way. All of them have brought me independence, mobility, and freedom to be the person I would like to be, and for me to achieve what I would like to. There is no reason why I can't achieve my dreams just because I can't see. Being blind is not a good enough reason to stop living and having a life.

So, to the four beautiful brown eyes in my life, Lola's and Woody's, I thank you from the bottom of my heart. You both bring so much to my life. The quality of my life is amazing because of you. Your genuineness and love is unconditional. I am so very grateful. I feel very blessed.

I hope you don't mind me reflecting and trying to explain to you what these two amazing animals have brought to my life and the amazing quality of life I have because of these two amazing animals. Okay I can't drive a car, but so what, I can do most other things. With my beautiful friends by my side, anything is possible.

So, take some time to think about the beautiful animals in your life, for what they bring to your life, the richness, the love, the happiness, the joy, the beauty. Perhaps you and I are similar, we agree that the gifts they give us are immeasurable.

*

JUST A MATTER OF TIME

Life

You know when things are going really really well there's that saying, about Murphy's Law, that you need to get ready the happy bubble will burst. Well, here it comes.

Yesterday started off wonderfully, really wow, wow, and wow. Then it fell in a heap!

Firstly, at some stage during the afternoon, we had a wee blackout. It lasted maybe a minute or two, but when it did come back on again it blew out our water pump from the bore which services the horse's water and our toilet and the garden. So, I find all this out when I go to mix Lola's feed. Hmm, no water to soak her feed. So, I come in and get the water out of the kitchen, no dramas easy-peasy.

I feed our beautiful Lola and then come in to get Matthew's dinner ready. I was busily preparing veggies when Matthew arrived home and says "put your hat on and come with me." He said it very calmly, which disturbed me immensely. He took my hand and in the other hand picked up my white cane, he guided me around the veranda. He then informed me that Lola was rolling and lying on the ground quite distressed. He took me down to the paddock and as soon as I called out to Lola, she called back to me and kept calling back to me. And then she stood up and I went to her, oh my heavens she was having a colic attack. So scary.

As you may know with colic, they sweat profusely. I removed Lola's rug, wet soggy rug that felt like I'd just got it out of the washing machine without spin drying it! It was saturated. Her breathing was horrible. She was stressed to the max, and all she wanted to do was cuddle and be beside me. I walked her up to my tack shed.

Holy cow, then the lightbulb moment. We have no water! So, God love Matthew trying to call the vet and at the same time bring water out for me. Matthews wonderful dad John came and held Lola while I sponged her bucket by bucket all over, trying to cool her down. Then she started frothing at the mouth and so Matthew syringed her mouth out with clean water from the kitchen and did this until the frothing stopped. Then hives came out all over her body. Holy cow! This was too much. Then to hear from one of the younger girls at our local Dubbo vets that no one was available to come out, "ring another vet" was to much.

Oh my heavens! I was panic stricken because Don, my vet, wasn't available, he wasn't there. He always looks after my horses, and to be told to find another vet absolutely busted me. I panicked.

Matthew rang another vet, but that vet was in surgery, so it meant more waiting. So I rang Don Crosby veterinary surgery back again and explained the situation once again. I explained she was frothing at the mouth and going into shock and she was now shaking all over. We were on the phone for ages waiting, waiting. On my heavens the waiting did my head in, and I was so stressed. My beautiful Lola was so, so uncomfortable and distressed.

The beautiful nurse kept talking to me and suggesting different things for us to do, which we did. These included Matthew syringing water into her mouth, getting her mouth clear, making sure there was no obstructions because they thought she may have been choking because she was frothing, but that wasn't the case. It must've been a side-effect of something, we have no idea. Then I was speaking to the vet, and they said someone would be there in the next 20 minutes. Oh my, doesn't time go so painfully slow when you are waiting, and you are worried about the health of your horse.

Matthew went out to the road to make sure the vet came down to where Lola and I were standing in the shade. Every now and again I walked her with my white cane. I didn't bring Woody into the situation as it was so stressful, and I didn't want him to pick up on my worry. Straight away when the amazing young vet Sara approached Lola, she spoke with confidence, and she was very thorough and took her time going over Lola.

We discussed what we thought may or may not have caused the colic episode and the hives. Oh my, Sara was amazing. She worked her magic and gave Lola three injections. One was an antihistamine, one was a mild painkiller, and if I remember correctly the other was a muscle relaxant, to help her stomach stop all the cramping and tension. Whatever that combination was it worked. Lola very quickly turned the corner. Phew!

I was so impressed with this wonderful young veterinarian's approach and bedside manner, plus the additional challenge of working with a client that's blind.

Okay, I know it, I might overreact a little bit when I'm super stressed. Sometime being blind truly sucks. Not being able to see what's going on magnifies everything. But Sarah was wonderful. She informed me, like Don does, about everything she was doing and why she was doing it. She told me when she was hearing for gut sounds, listening to Lola's lungs, checking her heartbeat, checking the pulses. Wow she was so very thorough. I must say other than when Don Crosby treats my horses I always worry when it's not Don. He is just so thorough and knows his job so well and always has the best interest of my horse or horses at the top of the list. In short – I trust him.

But I shouldn't have worried. Sara was amazing, so very thorough, passionate, interested, engaging and informative. I was super impressed. So I asked her, are you staying? We need someone when Don is not here that we can rely on. She then informed us that she's off to England. Oh no! In a heartbeat I was heartbroken. This beautiful girl is such a talented, caring, empathetic veterinarian who can communicate so effectively. Such vet of this calibre are few and far between, and she was also very knowledgeable. And we were going to lose her! No!

But, back to Lola.

Lola was slowly starting to feel better. We put a light cotton rug on her, and Matthew put her in her paddock and went and checked her every few hours, well so did my wonderful mother-in-law Lee.

We had all had such a stressful afternoon, my father-in-law John asked if we'd like fish and chips for dinner? It was yes please all-round, no one wanted to cook, which was just so good. During the evening everyone took turns to go check on Lola. When Lee was leaving at 11 pm to go home, they live next door, she firstly went down with a torch and gave Lola the once over. It was from that visit that we decided Lola could have a biscuit of hay. Which she really enjoyed.

In my life there is no 'I' in Team. We are never alone. There is always a team making it work for my beautiful horses and I.

The next morning was such a spectacular morning. Made even better by the sound that called out to me as I went down to the paddock, tapping my white cane as I went, all the while with the sun shining on my face from the East. Lola heard the tink, tink, tink of the cane and whinnied to me. It was so lovely. She was bright and bubbly and felt beautiful. I gave her the hard feed and then went back probably half an hour later and gave her a biscuit of the beautiful juicy lucerne hay that Matthew had grown and harvested.

I am so grateful that Lola is feeling better, so very grateful to the beautiful vet Sara for coming out and looking after and treating Lola. We are so at the mercy of having a good veterinarian here in Dubbo. I suspect it's the same anxiety for other small regional areas.

Such situations can be make-or-break – whether it be colic, snakebite or a leg injury. Deciding if that injury is retrievable or fixable all comes down to the availability of getting a vet. We feel so so grateful to Sara.

You can now understand why I hope Murphy stays away for a while. We still have no water. I can't wait to get the water on and give our beautiful Lola a bath plus that wash will be a good change for getting rid of the rest of the sand. Because

But I cannot emphasise enough how these things happened in my life yesterday. My wonderful husband, my amazing father-in-law, and my beautiful mother-in-law – they were all there beside me working with Lola and Sara the vet. It was a team effort, as per usual. But I am so grateful to have the most amazing family and the coolest parents in law ever. Oh my heavens, Lee and John are awesome. We dine together, we drink together and do cheese and bickies together. There are always loads of laughs. I feel just so grateful.

Now back to all thins Lola. She was so excited this morning when I was walking down to the paddock, I heard Lola calling me. This means she's happy and she's feeling good. She greeted me with a very big whinny then came and ate her breakfast. We have kept a close eye on her today, she is much brighter and seems to be recovered. I will take her for a quiet walk tomorrow just on the lead, no pressure, just let her go for a quiet walk and relax.

*

WHY, WHAT, WHERE AND WHEN?

"If it's going to be – it's up to me!"

Sue-Ellen Lovett

Live The Dream

WHAT DOES IT FEEL LIKE WHEN YOU ARE WALKING TO YOUR HORSE, TO GO WORK OR PLAY WITH THEM?

Oh, this is an easy question.

It's like that feeling you get on a spring day when a mischievous breeze wizzes around you and reminds us how wonderful it is to be alive.

I'm excited. So much happy anticipation. I'm outdoors playing with my animals.

Bring it on!

Why did you retire your last Guide Dog Armani and not replace her straight away?

This was no fault of Armani's. I wasn't going into town very often, and then the NDIS came along offering me someone that could take me shopping and to do other chores for me, with me. The NDIS providing me such support was totally liberating, not that using a Guide Dog wasn't. But the NDIS allowed me to have someone tell me what me was around, and what I was looking at. A Guide Dog can't do that.

Do you use a white cane?

Yes, I certainly do. I incorporate my Guide Dog and my white cane on the farm. I use my white cane for simple tasks, whereas I use Woody with my horse Lola and to guide me out to the dressage arena and more challenging tasks.

This is all done with such confidence, using my beautiful Guide Dog Woody.

How long have you had Guide Dogs for?

I received my first Guide Dog in 1981, her name was Donna. She was the first German Shepherd Guide Dog in Australia, and she was extremely intelligent.

Do you have a favourite Guide Dog?

Well, to be very honest, I did have a favourite Guide Dog. He stood out from all the others because he was so incredibly professional, and because he came into my life when I was travelling the world competing, I was very busy. He and I did so very much travel and spending time together. We went to Atlanta in 1996 to the

Paralympic Games, to the World Championships in Denmark in 1999, then the Sydney 2000 Paralympic Games and a huge number of fundraising events and being on different committees and Boards.

Beside me at all of it, was my beautiful Guide Dog Eccles.

He was my Suit and Tie guy; he was always so incredibly professional.

CAN YOU TAKE YOUR GUIDE DOG IN AN AEROPLANE?

Absolutely! My Guide Dog can fly anywhere with me in the world. That's as long as the country is accepting, and we go through all that countries quarantine procedures. When we return home to Australia, we have our own quarantine process to go through.

Typically, my Guide Dog goes into quarantine for a month when we fly back into Australia.

When we fly domestically within Australia, I can fly anywhere with my Guide Dog, no quarantine or restrictions apply. Typically, the airline give me an extra seat, but if not, my Guide Dog quietly crawls up under my legs and sleeps the entire trip.

CAN YOU CATCH A TAXI TOGETHER?

Yes, absolutely!
Guide Dogs are allowed on all public transport including taxis, planes, trains, trams, and buses. During a Guide Dogs training, they go on all these transports and do it with ease and create no problem for the public. Guide Dogs are exceptionally well mannered.

HAVE YOU BEEN REFUSED A RIDE IN A TAXI?

I am sorry to have to tell you the answer to this question.
I will always find this answer really sad. Yes, quite a few times, with

my different Guide Dogs. It has generally been caused because of the drivers lack of knowledge and a little bit of ignorance; I think.

There are lots of campaigns out there explaining Guide Dogs can go anywhere, including Taxis. So, there is no excuse for this driver ignorance.

WHAT DO YOU DO WHEN YOU GET REFUSED A RIDE IN A TAXI?

Firstly, I try to explain to the taxi driver that a Guide Dog IS ALLOWED in a taxi, and that it is an illegal act to refuse a Guide Dog and I a ride.

I also show them my card which is supplied to me by Guide Dogs explaining the legalities of refusing me a ride in the taxi.

If they still refuse, I get someone to write down the taxis number plate, and the phone number on the side of the cab, so I can ring Guide Dogs NSW office. After I report it to Guide Dogs, I then ring Human Rights and Equal Opportunities and report the discrimination act.

Firstly, such an act is so very humiliating, and embarrassing. But it is discriminatory to be refused a ride in a taxi.

Such an act is horrible and hurtful. It always has a very big impact on my confidence being refused a ride in a taxi. Sighted people don't get refused a ride.

WHEN YOU HAVE REPORTED TAXI DRIVERS TO GUIDE DOGS AND HUMAN RIGHTS AND EQUAL OPPORTUNITIES, WHAT DID YOU WANT OUT OF IT?

This is an easy one, I would like the taxi driver and the people who employ them and other taxi drivers to be educated about the rules around accessibility to Guide Dogs, and that it is discrimination to deny us a ride. I would also like an apology. I don't always get the apology.

I have had two cases that have gone to court; those taxi drivers received a fine and were banned from driving a taxi for six months.

WHAT ABOUT GOING TO RESTAURANTS, HOTELS, MOTELS, AND CAFES?

The conduct they are to provide is the same as for the taxis and other modes of transport. They cannot deny a Guide Dog and their handler access. We can dine at any restaurant, stay at any motel and go to any café. Our access to these venues should never be an issue.

When you and your Guide Dog go to a cafe or a restaurant, the Guide Dogs sits quietly at your side, by your chair. You wouldn't know they are there.

All Guide Dogs have wonderful manners. They don't jump around when food comes, they don't interact with anyone or impede anyone. They just sit quietly or sleep.

At some restaurants their staff make us feel so welcome they bring out a container of water for the Guide Dog. On hot days that container has some ice cubes in it! Boy oh boy do my dogs love the ice cubes.

HAVE YOU EVER BEEN REFUSED ACCESS TO A RESTAURANT, A MOTEL, OR A HOTEL?

Sadly yes.
What did you do when you were refused access to the restaurant, motel or hotel?

I have to admit that being refused access to these venues has had a profound effect on me.

Imagine how you'd feel when you go to do a simple thing like walk into a restaurant, motel or hotel, and they stop you, they tell you NO!

Being refused access is not just embarrassing and upsetting, it has a massive effect on your confidence and your preparedness to going out in public in the future.

Over the years I have had many refusals. While a lot of them I was able to talk around after I educated them about Guide Dogs being able to go into restaurants, cafes, hotels, motels, etc.

But there have been the odd occasion where no amount of explanation or attempted education has worked. On those occasions I had to escalate the situation to contact Guide Dogs NSW head office and reporting the venues breach of law.

Then I ring Human Rights and Equal Opportunities and submit a formal complaint.

WHAT ARE YOU EXPECTING TO ACHIEVE OUT OF REPORTING THE MOTEL, HOTEL, RESTAURANT OR CAFE OWNER?

Firstly I report them to Guide Dogs head office in NSW. They then approach the offending venue directly, giving them the information they need to know about discrimination and that it is illegal to refuse a Guide Dog and their handler access to their venue.

By going to Human Rights and Equal Opportunities I hope for three outcomes: number one is that the offending place gets a letter from Human Rights and Equal Opportunities explaining that their conduct is illegal, and discriminatory to refuse access to a Guide Dog and their handler.

Number two is that the offending place attend training with Guide Dogs, about Guide Dogs being able to have access to their venue, and that it is illegal to refuse them.

Number three is an apology written by the offending person. I think this is really important. They need to understand how hurtful and how humiliating it is to be refused access. That their refusal typically happens in public, them coming to the entrance and stopping me from entering, makes it twice as bad.

WHAT HAPPENS IF YOU DON'T
GET AN APOLOGY?

This has happened only once. Getting that apology kept going backwards and forwards from the restaurant owner through Human Rights and Equal Opportunities, and they kept getting a letter done by the solicitor. This was a beautifully written letter, but it was missing something. The owner refused to acknowledge the fact that they had refused me access to their restaurant.

So back and forwards it continued, for ages. The wonderful person at Human Rights and Equal Opportunities pointed out to me that they thought the restaurant owner was anxious about saying any version of "I'm sorry, I did the wrong thing, I should have let you in" that I'd sue him.

My reply to yet another incomplete letter, was that if he didn't send me a written apology, a proper apology, I would sue him.

That afternoon I received the most beautifully written letter from the offending gentleman. All is forgiven. It's okay, I just wanted him to realise that my Guide Dog and I can go and visit his restaurant any time and it will be fine.

Finally, it was a good outcome all round.

DO YOU ENJOY TRAINING WITH
A NEW GUIDE DOG?

Oh, my heavens absolutely!
I have just finished training with my beautiful new Guide Dog Woody, and it has been totally awesome.

Our Guide Dog trainer Danni was amazing. We had particular new skills all nutted out in about four days, half the time she expected. It was totally awesome.

Do you use your Guide Dog on the farm?

My last six Guide Dogs I never used on the farm. I was always to scared of them being bitten by a brown snake. So, I just battled through with my white cane.

But in the last year or so my orientation skills have gotten really bad. I get lost in our garden... a lot! It became almost routine for me to end up in the arms of the prickly lemon tree, in the rosemary bush or colliding with a low hanging branch.

I really needed some help. By using my Guide Dog on the farm, oh my heavens, voila, my orientation is fixed straight away.

Woody's destination work is totally amazing. He works in wonderful straight lines, goes around things when he needs to, so we go from point A to point B effortlessly.

Do you think Guide Dog Woody likes working on the farm?

Yes, absolutely. I truly think Woody loves working on the farm. He also loves leading my horse Lola and I from point A to point B, like from the Tack Shed out to the Dressage arena. He loves sitting in his kennel chewing on his bone while I train Lola.

I'm so happy he is happy. The independence for me and the freedom he provides certainly makes me happy. It's totally awesome.

Have any of your Guide Dogs died before they retired?

Oh yes, and it was so sad. My beautiful Guide Dog Donna the German Shepherd died of cancer after I had her for only a short time, about 5 years. This was devastating.

Donna was my first taste of independence and mobility. Her by my side was liberating, it was amazing, and oh how it hurt when she died.

WHEN DONNA DIED, DID YOU GET A NEW GUIDE DOG?

Yes, I did, but it was so very hard.

All I wanted was Donna back. But I had to keep putting one foot in front of the other and moving forward.

I trained with a lovely little golden Labrador bitch called Tara. She was a great Guide Dog, and I felt so sad when I retired her at the age of 11. Why did I feel sad? Because I still had Donna embedded in my heart when I got Tara. I needed a Guide Dog for my independence and mobility, but I missed Donna so very much.

But you must keep moving forward. And Tara was a wonderful Guide Dog.

HAVE ALL YOUR GUIDE DOGS BEEN THE SAME?

Oh heavens, no. They are all individuals.

They have all been trained the same way to be a Guide Dog, but they each have their own personality and their own little idiosyncrasies. I think those unique bits of their character is what makes them so special.

WHEN YOU ARE WORKING WITH YOUR GUIDE DOG AND WERE TRAINING WITH DANNI, DID YOU USE TREATS TO REWARD WOODY?

Oh, my heavens, this is a super question.

I had never used treats before, not even with one of my other six Guide Dogs. Why? Because I know the Labrador in the Guide Dog looooves food. They by their very breeding labs have a tendency to have food distraction issues. Plus, I thought that giving a Guide Dog a treat would exacerbate that food distraction glitch.

Well, welcome Woody! He quickly put a stop to this misunderstanding. I have used treats with his training, his destination work and everything has happened so much quicker. I don't give him a treat every time, and it is getting less and less, but it has been an amazing way to achieve goals and have them embedded in the Guide Dogs so much quicker than just using praise.

Don't get me wrong, praise alone does work. But using a treat to reward that correct behaviour works quicker and is as effective. And yes, it's not about Woody, or any animals training, being quick! It is about being efficient and getting a job done well.

WHAT DO YOU DO WITH YOUR GUIDE DOGS WHEN THEY RETIRE?

Well, there is never a lack of people who would like my retired Guide Dogs. It's a matter of choosing a home where you think your Guide Dog would be the happiest. My Guide Dogs have all retired to beautiful homes. The people haven't always kept in contact with me to let me know when my dog has passed away. But that's okay, as long as the Guide Dogs have had a wonderful retirement, I'm happy.

DO YOU VISIT YOUR GUIDE DOGS AFTER THEY RETIRE?

No. When my dogs are retired to a life with someone else looking after them, I say goodbye to them.

I think it is very important that my Guide Dog now has a new home and new people to care for them and love them. I don't want to interfere with that bonding process and them being happy.

WAS IT AN ADVANTAGE MEETING WOODY FOR A COUPLE OF HOURS IN MID-DECEMBER 2021?

Oh, wow! Yes!

And Woody remembered so many things which was so cool. When Hayley brought him to visit me last December, we spent about two hours in the garden. We went for a walk, I had a trial of him in hand, we did a little bit of destination work following

Matthew. And boy of boy was I extra excited about Woody coming to live with us very soon.

Woody forgot nothing! He was totally awesome!

But I knew when I met him, we were meant to be.

WHAT IS SO DIFFERENT ABOUT WOODY?

What a great question. I've given it a lot of thought.
I think having met him a month before we started training was a big advantage. I knew who I was letting into my heart and who I was going to be working with. 'But I continually say this amazing Guide Dog Woody has a certain amount of magic about him. He has to be the happiest Guide Dog I have ever had. I can feel it in the air. And from that very short meeting when he was brought him to the farm for us to meet, I knew we were meant to be. I already knew Woody was going to be an amazing Guide Dog.

WHAT IS THE BEST THING GUIDE DOGS BRING TO YOUR LIFE?

Wow, wow, and wow! This is an easy one; independenc,e mobility, freedom, the ability to do whatever I like, to live my best life and have my best mate by my side. I am so very grateful to my beautiful Guide Dogs. What they have brought to my life. Every time I think about them, I smile and when I am working with Woody, we are both smiling.

I love not getting lost in the garden.

I love not running into the prickly Lemon Tree. I love not getting bitten by the electric fence through my white cane.

Woody has brought a lot of confidence and freedom back into my life. Woody you totally rock!

WHERE ARE SOME OF THE COOL PLACES YOU AND YOUR GUIDE DOGS HAVE BEEN?

With my Guide Dogs I have travelled extensively overseas, especially with beautiful Guide Dog Eccles.

I have taken my Guide Dogs with me on my long-distance rides, which have raised over $3.2 MILLION for various charities.

We have visited many amazing places like Parliament House in Canberra, and the Opera House in Sydney, many times. With my Guide Dogs I was also an Australia Day Ambassador for 21 years; this was an amazing experience. I was also on the Board of the Sydney Paralympic Games appointed by Michael Knight. This meant flying to Sydney every couple of weeks for board meetings. This was an awesome experience, loads of flying time with my Guide Dog Eccles.

I really think when it comes down to it, every day is an adventure with my Guide Dogs. We have the privilege of doing many amazing things.

*

LEARNING CURVE

"One Step At A Time"

What a spectacular day we're having. Plus we had some beautiful rain overnight, 18 mils that was accompanied by lots of thunder and lightning.

I've had a busy few days with Lola being sick but can now relax knowing she is over her colic. She's better and we have water in the tanks, thank heavens.

This morning was particularly hectic with our amazing farrier Troy Lomax coming to shoe Lola and Lee's mare Sophie. I always love it when Troy and his dad visit, we have such interesting conversations.

I nearly did a new destination for Woody this morning. I could have a word for getting him to take Lola and I down to Lee's stables to have Lola shod. But I thought I should do the destination with Matthew first, that way Woody gets to follow Matthew and have a queue to go to. So, I tapped on down with my white cane. Troy came and got me halfway down and took Lola for me which was wonderful. Then I went and had a cuppa with my wonderful mother-in-law Lee. That's always so much fun.

After I had lunch, I thought well now we have water, woohoo! I am going to give my beautiful Lola a wash. So, Woody and I headed off down to get Lola. This was going really well until oops, what happened was my fault, not Woody's.

I was so disappointed, but I shouldn't have been, I didn't follow protocol and tie Woody up when Lola came up to me, to catch her.

So, this is how it played out. Woody must've spotted Thunder Paws in the garden. Well holy hell! He was gone in a flash chasing our pussycat up onto the veranda. I heard yelling and Thunder Paws going crook. I put Lola back in her paddock and off I went to try and retrieve Woody. I had to find him first!

All of this mess though was my fault. I should have tethered him at the paddock gate, which I had been doing. But he had been so good, so amazing, I cut corners and didn't. Him running off after Thunder Paws, doing something he shouldn't, is exactly what happens when you don't follow protocol and skip steps in a certain sequence.

So, I found Woody and proceeded back down to Lola's gate. Yes, I tied him up this time while I caught Lola, then he guided Lola and I to the tack shed.

There I gave Lola a lovely brush and a wash with my wonderful Doctor Show shampoo. Oh, she smelt amazing and when she dried, she felt so shiny. Woody sat quietly by his drum, tied to the drum. But I think he knew I was disappointed in him. But he didn't miss a beat guiding me. Oh my heavens he is the most amazing Guide Dog.

This was a very big lesson for me. Even though he is so amazing I shouldn't have cut corners. He's still in training and only quite young. If I had tethered him at the gate, he would not have ran after the pussycat. So, guess what, I will be tethering him at the gate from now on. So, this is the first cross in Woody's training. He is such a good boy, and I think he thought it was just a big game. He wasn't trying to hurt Thunder Paws. He just wanted to play. But he's yet to learn that while he's in harness, he must concentrate on what I'm doing, not run off and go play!

So, from now on I will concentrate on doing the right thing by my Guide Dog and not skip steps.

After Lola was washed and smelling beautiful, we took her back down to her paddock and let her go. We went back to the tack shed and I tethered Woody to the drum. I put away all the washing equipment and got Lola's dirty rugs and put them in the washing machine. I feel so disappointed in myself for letting Woody down with my inconsistency. I trusted him to much, he wasn't ready yet. It was wrong of me to think he wouldn't move.

Yes, huge learning curve for the Blind Chick today.

I'm excited about tomorrow; Woody and I are planning on catching Lola and taking her to do some work in the dressage arena.

I think the biggest thing that has come out of today, and it's true for whatever 'other' you are working with, be that a person or an animal, your horse, or your Guide Dog; consistency and setting things up for no one to fail is critical.

Yes, I let my end down, but I will not do it again. And I'm still super proud of Woody. After that hiccup we just continued on, he worked so well.

*

SETTING UP FOR SUCCESS

Make every day count

I am often reminded about that amazing saying our beautiful Johno used to harp on with – "Take one step at a time." By doing one step at a time, you have time to think, and you have time to set yourself up for success. Today that was my goal. I was planning on riding, but it's overcast and no sun. So while we still went and caught our beautiful Lola and worked her, we couldn't ride today.

This is how I set up for success this morning. Bum bag for Lola with carrots as treats. Bum bag for Woody with his treats. I think this is a good start for success. I went out onto the veranda, and as soon as I reach for the Guide Dog harness Woody is very excited. He loves his work. I proceed to put his harness on and asked him to sit, then up and stand. Oops! I realised what I'd done as soon as I went to take up the harness. Oh heavens, I had put it on back to front. The handle part was over his nose! This would never work. So, I re-harnessed Woody, thank heavens he is patient.

But I must say, I did have a quite giggle to myself. Thank heavens no one saw what I'd done. In the 40 years of having a Guide Dog that was the first time this has ever happened. Once I had the harness on the right way, Woody and I proceeded to the tack shed where I got the grooming gear and Lola's work boots out ready. Then Woody and I went down to Lola's paddock. While I was off catching Lola, Woody was tethered at the gate. This is what I should have done yesterday.

After I caught Lola, I unhooked Woody from the gate and said, "to the tack shed Woody." And he guided Lola and I up to the tack shed. I tethered Woody at his drum, and he sat and watched me take Lola's rugs off and give her a lovely big brush. She smelt divine after her wash yesterday, her tail felt like silk. After a lovely brush, I put Lola's leg boots on and Woody guided her and I out to the dressage arena.

I changed my command a little bit today. I asked Woody to go to his kennel, which he did straightaway. When we got out to the arena, I took off his harness and hooked him up at his kennel and gave him a bone to chew. To which he seemed pretty happy. Lola and I then went into the dressage arena. I was using the lunge whip as a white cane to find the gateway. We walked in and then, oopsy! Someone forgot it had been raining and there was mud, there was water, but we were in it already. So, we mosey on through to an area of the arena where there was no mud. I proceeded to give Lola a lovely big walk and just make sure she was sounding and feeling ok after her colic episode.

I did 20 minutes either side, walk, trot, and canter. Lots of transitions, lots of winding her in, lots of canter pirouette exercises. It was a lovely session. For the first 10 minutes I could hear Woody busily eating his bone in the kennel. I had one ear on what Lola was doing, and one ear on listening for Woody. Then things went quiet! I kept thinking, oh my heavens I hope he hasn't gotten off his chain at his kennel. But I thought, no, it's a good chain, he'll be fine. But the reality was, I couldn't hear him.

This worried me a little. Keep in mind I couldn't just have a glance at the kennel to see if he was there. As it was, I went to the wrong end of the arena to exit, because there was no sun. After a wonderful session working Lola, I walked around the dressage arena with the lunge whip as my white cane and found the exit, I took the lunge lead off Lola and went over to Woody.

Woody proudly came out of his kennel and stood while I put the harness on the right way round this time! When I asked Woody to go back to the tack shed, oh my heavens, it felt so good. I just so wanted to have a video to show you all how confident we were this morning. Totally awesome! And Woody's Guide Dog work was exceptional.

When we arrived to the tack shed he went straight to his drum, on which I tethered him. Then I took Lola's boots off and gave her a big brush and put a clean rug on her. The dirty needed to be washed. Woody then guided Lola and I down to her paddock. I tethered Woody at the gate, did the carrot stretching exercises with Lola, then let her go. What a spectacular morning.

Woody and I then went back to the tack shed, I cleaned up a few things, then we went back to the house and went inside.

I'm so proud of Woody and my beautiful Lola. We can train by ourselves. It feels amazing!

I know I didn't ride, but that's okay. It's one of those steps Johno talks about. We only lunged today, but we might ride tomorrow if there is sunshine. How cool is it when you set up for success and just do one step at a time to get there.

*

THE HORSE IN THE PICTURE

Left to right: Johno, Mudgee, Hectic

THANK YOU.

Thank you for giving me vision when I cannot see.

Thank you for teaching me to listen with my heart.

Thank you for teaching me to feel and to listen.

Thank you for teaching me to be present and in the moment and about being accountable.

Thank you for teaching me how to turn frustration into elation and triumph and joy.

Thank you for being my confidant, and listening to my innermost secrets, and comforting me when I am down.

Thank you for being the wind beneath my wings, helping me to soar to great heights.

Thank you for helping me show my ability, not my disability.

Thank you for accepting me just the way I am.

Thank you for teaching me to listen, to take time to enjoy our moments in time.

Thank you for never sitting in judgement.

Thank you for teaching me there is another way.

Thank you for just being you, my beautiful horse.

The horses in these pictures are all angels now.

I have our beautiful memories locked deep in my heart.

I am so grateful for the time we spent together.

So grateful for the memories we made.

So grateful for the memories to be made.

The horses in these pictures, thank you for coming into my life and making it richer

Thank you for teaching me.

I feel so grateful, so humbled, so blessed.

The horses in the pictures - I humbly thank you.

Sue-Ellen Lovett

*

REFLECTION

Mudgee, Eccles & The Blind Chick

I am so very blessed and grateful for the magnificent horses that have touched my life.

My beautiful horses Mudgee, Hectic, Ko-Olina, Desiderata, Cascador, Johno, Lola, Blue & Ollie, to name a few. There has been so many more. And many new cherished memories to be made.

I feel so very blessed and grateful.

*

LOVELY LESSON

Take the time it takes

Since Lola got in trouble with colic, I have been very slowing bringing her back into work.

I've only been working her three or four times since that colic episode. She's got her new dancing shoes on, the farrier came yesterday, so today a friend came for a lesson on her. It was awesome! Each time my friend steps up that much more, and she's such a lovely rider. My friend and I are so on the same page, we are starting to say the same things at the same time. It's really funny.

Today we worked again on transitions, coming back from the canter to the trot, or the canter to the walk, not using your hands, slowing your seat, slowing your seat, sitting tall, and walk. All the same can be done from the canter to the trot, but not with your hands, otherwise it's abrupt and often not free and flowing. It has been wonderful listening to my friend as she talks to Lola and the penny drops for my friend. She must be super proud of herself today, some of the transitions from one gait to another were spectacular.

We also worked on collection, and the difference between a collected walk and a long rein walk. Working on doing a transition without Lola shortening her stride and the rhythm and regularity changing too much. The rhythm and regularity should not change when you do a transition within a pace. And oh my heavens, I'm now doing the most amazing leg yields. I'm keeping my body parallel with the long side of the arena.

It is so lovely giving someone lessons that is thirsty for information. This lovely lady is taking all that she is learning on me back to help her Australian Stockhorse. I'm told that I'm going so much better than weeks ago when I first arrived, which is so cool. We talked a lot about position, sitting tall, not leaning forward, and that you must engage your seat so you can bring the energy through from the back and into your hand. "Ride the horse through into the bridle" is a constant message in my head.

The lady and I did some lovely extended trots, once she realised she had to use her seat more. "Sit tall, look up, shoulders back" this helped Lola come through from behind. I could hear the difference in the rhythm and sound of her foot falls each stride, impacting the sand floor of the arena.

That was excellent! But as we know, old habits are hard to get rid of. I know personally I have a couple of them that I have had for 20 years. My coaches will always say the same thing about my right hand. It's just one of those things, but it's something I keep working at.

I think Lola loves it when my friend rides her. They are a very relaxed, confident, and a competent rider, plus... quite chilled. No pressure. This suits Lola down to the ground. We also worked on doing movements at a certain position in the arena, and reinforcing the importance of when you ask for something and it's not done till four strides later, that's not acceptable.

We also did some circle work and how to work out whether you are correct when you are doing a 15-meter circle. How much bend do I have for a 15-meter circle. It was really cool.

All the time while this lesson was going on, beautiful Woody who had guided me out to the dressage arena, was sitting in his kennel chewing on a bone. Hilarious was he did not come out until I called him out. I think he quite likes his Woody kennel.

*

FINDING THE ELUSIVE UNICORN

Meet Ollie. It's hard to tell who is smiling more, him, me or our Blind Chick!

Well, I am sure this blindness gig is not an easy path to tread, especially when you put having horses in your life into the equation. Plus competing with that horse!

I know that the past few years have been really quite difficult for my Blind Chick. Losing a horse is tough, then trying to find a new one, the right one, one that has the temperament a Blind Chick needs is not an easy duet.

The last amazing dressage horse my Blind Chick was able to compete on she retired about five years ago. His name was Desiderata. He was a magnificent dance partner and travelled with her far and wide with the help of one of her amazing sponsors. The person who helped my Blind Chick and Desiderata, Desi for short, go to the dizzying heights of doing a grand prix dressage demonstration at Willinga Park and many other events, was a lovely gentleman called Terry Snow. Riding at Terry's Willinga Park, on the coast of New South Wales, south west of Canberra, was a highlight in my Blind Chick's riding career. And that's certainly high praise given she's competed internationally, even at World Championships in Denmark! Not only did they get to ride a Grand Prix test, but that demonstration ride in front of a packed crowd in the magnificent, covered arena was so powerful, there wasn't a dry eye in sight.

When my Blind Chick decided to retire Desiderata, that decision was massive. She didn't want to keep working him at such a high level when he already had arthritic changes when she brought him. She didn't want Desi to stick around if every month he was requiring a large nursing team to do the routine of supporting his soundness.

Not only was retiring Desi a massive decision, his departure left an amazingly big gap in her life.

Between my Blind Chick and her lovely mother-in-law Lee, many, many hours were spent looking through web pages and Facebook posts for that elusive unicorn. My Blind Chick's phone reads her the ads, ones she thought were suitable she'd forward to Lee for her to have a look at photos, videos, etc. This was a long and tedious process but... but they came across a potential perfect fit, a horse called Johno.

Johno and the Blind Chick had this incredible relationship, and no, she was not put off by his height 18.3 hands high (1.9 metres). He looked after the Blind Chick so well, and in her heart, she felt she could not live without him.

Well, there is quite a story to the buying of Jono. To find out more about that whole other adventure, grab a copy of Johno and the Blind Chick I and II. It shares their incredible story from how husband Matthew purchased Johno for his wife, not knowing Johno had a neurological condition called Equine Shivers! Yes.

Even though Johno had passed the vet check and was deemed fit for the dressage purpose the Blind Chick wanted him for.

From the get-go some people noticed Johno had some quirky habits, like how he found walking backwards quite difficult, but it wasn't until three months into their life together that his Equine Shivers condition was diagnosed. This made it very difficult for Johno on a day-to-day basis as his brain did not always have the ability to talk to his hind legs and then eventually his front legs. He progressed to having what can only be described as having episodes when he went from a normal horse to having a massive brain explosion. Those explosion episodes were things he couldn't control and yes, at times they were dangerous to be around. Any horse that can't control their own outbursts is bad enough, but when you're totally blind and that horse is a giant like Johno, that's a game changer.

My Blind Chick was incredible in researching all she could about Equine Shivers and arranging the best care routine for Johno. He was still able to be ridden as his episodes were being so well managed. Until one day he had an episode of such magnitude he behaved out of character and bucked. That wouldn't have been such a problem if my Blind Chick hadn't been riding him! She was thrown and broke her knee!

This was devastating for my Blind Chick. It was the start of the realisation that Johno was not going to get better, his Equine Shivers was getting worse. It progressed quite quickly from that day. His behaviour became more unreliable and very unstable. Even to lead him in the paddock he could, without warning, rear and have adverse reactions to the simplest stimuli.

So, after a period of only two years and two days, all the vets and specialists that had been part of Johno's team, trying their best to as a minimum, to help halt the progress of the Shivers and give Johno a quality of life without his dangerous outbursts, sadly, unanimously, they decided to euthanise Johno for his own safety, and for the safety of my Blind Chick. They had no alternative. If they didn't someone could get hurt way more than a busted knee.

Would you like to know more about Johno and the Blind Chick? As I mentioned earlier, it's an incredible journey. If you'd like to know the full story, there are two books: Johno & The Blind Chick 1 & 2. Just go to www.TheBlindChick.com.au.

Then along came the amazing Lola. Having her was an awesome opportunity for the Blind Chick. This lovely mare had loads of experience, had competed successfully in various sports and was super nice to be with.

But keep in mind my Blind Chick has absolutely no sight at all, and as time with Lola went on, she realised that her confidence post that Johno roller coaster wasn't as high as it used to be. She described it to me as feeling like she was riding Lola with the handbrake on all the time. I get why this bothered her, big time. She didn't want to stall Lola's progress, or stop Lola's chance to go out and compete, to collect loads of ribbons, and to have fun.

In mulling over her feelings and what to do about Lola, she was reminded of a question a wonderful friend had asked her. It was simple, but incredibly powerful and to the point - "Are you having fun with your horse?" She knew by how quickly she answered that question what she had to do.

So it was with a very sad heart that my Blind Chick sold Lola. She is an incredible horse but... for where my Blind Chick's confidence was at that time, Lola had way too much natural zoom zoom for my Blind Chick. This was an extremely hard time for my Blind Chick, coming to the realisation that she wasn't back to her normal confident self, yet.

I think she went through a very dark time with these realisations.

I think one of the hardest things is being honest to yourself, and she certainly was.

Unlike us who have sight, we have a lot more wiggle room when making decisions like this. Do we keep a horse for a bit longer, or not at all. But wrong decisions for my Blind Chick about such things like should she persevere with that particular horse, or not, can be fatal, catastrophic or just plain not fun for her. She had to be honest. Whether she liked it or not.

And boy oh boy... she was!

Now you can better understand why I love, love, love my Blind Chick. She's tough in ways people shouldn't have to be. And she keeps doing that 'one step at a time' in the right direction.

What happened next I've abbreviated for you, made the story a little shorter. Lola was sold to a wonderful home and as an interim to getting a dressage horse again, my Blind Chick decided to get a horse she could just play with for a while. A horse she didn't have to progress up the grades training it to be her next competition horse. She wanted a horse she could have fun with, just play with for a while.

Along came... Blue!

Oh wow he's gorgeous. I met him. That's him on the front cover. He's 14.2 hands high, grey and loads of fun. She rode him bareback in a halter like she used to when she was a kid. He was exactly what she needed, at that time.

But you can't take someone's innate who they are, what's in their DNA, out of them. And as time went on my Blind Chick realised while Blue was no pressure, and lots of fun, she needed to get back to what she love, love, loved. So, she made the decision to sell little Blue. Now I don't think this was a hard decision, but I do think it was this decision that helped her realise Blue had indeed helped a big chunk of her confidence to return. And with that return she could now get back to fulfilling her dreams and what she really wanted to be doing.

What did she really want to be doing you ask? She wanted to be riding a dressage horse, a horse that had been there and done that. A horse that was reliable and sensible. It didn't have to have a lot of education as she loves training horses. (And she's fantastic at it).

So, the hunt was on for that veritable Unicorn!

The first thing my Blind Chick did was put together a list of the things she'd like in her next horse. Then she put a post on her Facebook page that she was looking and set about trolling through loads of adverts and websites to see what she could find.

Her two amazing coaches, Jenelle Waters, and Jacqueline Benn gave her strict instructions that this time she was not to buy another horse without them being with her, and making sure it was perfect for her. Yippee, everyone was now helping look for that elusive Unicorn.

Jacqueline and Jenelle found a few horses that looked suitable, they spoke with the various owners at length, they watched videos, got photos and slowly but slowly whittled down the potential new horse list to guess how many horses?

Just one!

It was a long trip down to Cootamundra, 4 hours each way, filled with anticipation. They drove all that way with the horse float on, just in case this horse was worthy of bringing home. What will this handsome big gelding be like? Will he have the right temperament for my Blind Chick and not go mental when she's tap tap tapping her white cane about? Will he be quiet enough? I know they didn't want to worry about all those things because the horse wasn't coming home if it didn't satisfy Jenelle and Jacqueline.

Well, when they got down to Cootamundra, they went straight out to the racecourse. This is where the possible elusive Unicorn was living.

Your friend

Woody

Guide Dog Extraordinaire

*

MEETING A UNICORN

Ollie, I & Janelle

Jenelle drove all the way down to Cootamundra with Jacqueline nursing a very sore back in the back seat, my Blind Chick in the front seat. They had a few stops on the way down to help minimise Jacqueline's backpain.

Now, here is what I was told happened when they arrived at the Cootamundra racecourse. They were met by a wonderful lady called Natalie and her husband Richie, who took them over to the stable to meet the prospective horse.

Jacqueline guided my Blind Chick to the fence. There were five people at that fence line and guess who the horse went to? Yes! He walked straight to my Blind Chick, not anybody else. Understandably my Blind Chick was totally delighted and so excited.

Jacqueline then guided my Blind Chick down to the gate and guided her through and she caught the horse. Hello Ollie! He is 16 hh (1.62m) high and brown with beautiful big soft eyes.

With Jacqueline's help, my Blind Chick lead Ollie into the stable block where they started putting his brushing boots on and saddling him. While that was going on my Blind Chick just kept touching Ollie all over, feeling him, getting to know his body, seeing if she could pick up any scars, seeing if he was sensitive or tender anywhere.

This getting to know you stuff is so important. Especially when you can't see!

After a bit of time, brushing and tacking Ollie up, they went out into the round yard. Jenelle rode him first, and he was very good. After Jenelle walked, trotted and cantered him in the round yard it was the big moment. Time for my Blind Chick to get on! Ouch, she hit her kneecap heaps of times on the round yard as they rode around as her orientation was a little off, but it was all good.

After my Blind Chick's ride, Janelle took Ollie out and rode him in the bigger area. She did some beautiful walk, trot, canter and loads of transitions. He was a little resistant at first to what she was asking him to do, but that's understandable given he was getting to know two new riders. He was also resistant with my Blind Chick in the upward transitions, wanting to hollow a little, but apparently this is a minor problem. I'm a Guide Dog so all this stuff is new to me.

Well, I must say there was one excited Blind Chick and two pretty happy coaches. Jenelle and Jacqueline were extremely happy and spoke to Natalie a lot about how important her full disclosure and honesty about this amazing horse needed to be as he would be for their blind friend, everything had to be so right.

So they had loads to talk about that night.

They asked Natalie about her recommendations for where to go for dinner and off they went back to the motel. They detoured first to get some champagne of course and nibblies then went back to the motel to have a wee celebration. The local Cootamundra pub was walking distance from their motel, so off they went for dinner. Well, apparently, they danced the night away, had a cracker of a night and where all very excited about riding Ollie again the next day.

They got out to the Cootamundra racecourse very early on the Sunday morning as it was a very long drive back home. Jenelle rode Ollie first out in the big yard. She went through his gaits; walk, trot and canter, he went very kindly. Then it was our Blind Chick's turn. She didn't canter, she walked and trotted and did loads of transitions. As you can imagine, riding a horse you don't know in a very big arena and not knowing where you're going, she could've been very nervous. She should've been nervous! But no! Ollie and my Blind Chick had an awesome ride, he was so good for her. The transitions were lovely and soft. My Blind Chick didn't push him a lot, she was happy to go just one step at a time.

She did loads of transitions; walk back to trot, back to walk, keeping a consistent contact and inside leg into that steady outside rein. I think my Blind Chick was in her element.

Yes, they paid for the elusive unicorn, he walked onto the float and off home they headed. I think everyone was very content and happy with the purchase of the wonderful Ollie.

Since Ollie has been home here on the farm with us in Dubbo, I've worked with him many times. But our first couple of times were under the watchful eye of Jenelle and Jacqueline. They helped ensure Ollie was fine with me, and fine with me guiding my Blind Chick. Those initial introductions went off without a hitch. This was a very exciting time I must say.

And I recognised while it was important for me, and important for Ollie that we all get alone, the three of us so happy together was a milestone moment for my Blind Chick. She was now one step closer to getting back to the life she loved; having me to guide her and having a dressage horse to train, ride and perhaps compete on one day.

But I must say I do get most upset when my Blind Chick goes out and works Ollie without me! Yes, she uses the white cane instead of me. I think she does this because it's a little quicker, and also it only happens on the days when the girls (Jenelle and Jacqueline) aren't here. So going alone to spend time with Ollie is exactly what they need, time to just hang out and get to know each other. While it is still early days, they're having so much fun together.

When she returns to the house I can tell how happy she is. Even her skin seems to tingle with the excitement of her now being able to live her best life again.

She has progress quite quickly with him and now can take Ollie out to the dressage arena by herself. My Blind Chick and I can catch Ollie in the paddock together, then I lead her to the tack shed where she tacks him up, then we mosey on out to the dressage arena. This is such cool fun, it's awesome being a farm dog you know. Plus, I have a new mate in Ollie. We love working together and it is so cool watching my Blind Chick get her confidence back, and watch Ollie and my Blind Chick's partnership grow.

I'm super excited about what the future for us, the three musketeers, will be. Watch this space!

Your friend

Woody

Guide Dog Extraordinaire

*

EYES

Thank You

EYES

By Sue-Ellen Lovett

You have beautiful golden eyes to see for me.
You give me freedom and mobility.

With your two golden eyes, you guide and keep me safe.
With your two golden eyes, we have freedom, independence
and mobility.

I gently hold your harness, and you guide me through each
day of my life.
You guide me down to catch my two beautiful brown horse
eyes.
You guide us through the garden.
You take us to the tack shed, where I saddle, and bridle my
two beautiful brown eyes.
Then my two beautiful golden eyes, you guide us out to the
dressage arena.

It is freedom, it is independence, it is life changing.

My two beautiful golden eyes, you sit quietly in your Woody
house while I mount my two beautiful brown eyes.

I now have wings, and we can fly, and soar.

Nobody knows my secret, that I can't see.

It's just a secret between you and me.

With my two beautiful golden eyes and two beautiful brown
eyes I am just like everyone else.

You both give me freedom, independence, mobility, and the
ability to be just like everyone else.

I thank you my beautiful horse, and my amazing Guide Dog.
You're just being you, and bringing me a quality of life I would
not have without you.

I am so blessed to have you both in my life.

God bless you Guide Dog Woody and my beautiful horse Ollie.

It's just a secret that I can't see because you both give me
vision.

Vision is much more than seeing.

Dedicated to my beautiful horse Ollie and my Guide Dog Woody

*

THANK YOU WOODY

THANK YOU WOODY

You are certainly no normal dog!
You were bred for a special job.
You were born to lead.

Woody, I thank you for being brave and courageous.
I thank you for your beautiful personality.
You bubble with enthusiasm when you work.
I thank you for your golden eyes that keep me safe.
You guide me and give me mobility; you care for me.

Yippee no more getting lost in the garden,
no more running into the prickly Lemon tree!

I admire your intelligence and your love of learning.
Your attitude brings us both so much joy and happiness when
we are together learning something new.

I thank you for the confidence you share with me as you guide
me around the farm and out to the dressage arena where I can
train my lovely horse.

I thank you for just being you,
my beautiful friend Woody,
my Guide Dog,
my eyes.

The Blind Chick

*

You never know what's around the corner.

It could be everything.

Or it could be nothing.

You keep putting one foot in front of the other,

and then...

one day you look back, and you've climbed a mountain!

Tom Hiddleston

Don't lose hope when it gets
dark, the stars will come out

Just one step at a
time is all it takes.
Look at me now!
Baby Woody
©MegRose Photography

*

*

Come Join Us on Facebook

www.facebook.com/JohnoAndTheBlindChick

&

www.facebook.com/SueEllen.Lovett

*

www.TheBlindChick.com.au

*

*

Front & Back Cover Design
Matt J Pike
www.mattpike.co

Front Cover Image
Guide Dog Woody, Blue & The Blind Chick
©MegRose Photography
www.megrosephotos.wixsite.com/mysite

Various Images
©MegRose Photography
www.megrosephotos.wixsite.com/mysite

©Prue Crichton
www.2CPhotography.com.au

©Noni McCarthy
www.SixtyByTwenty.com.au

©Guide Dogs NSW   ©Dannielle Hogan

©Debra Lovett   ©Jacqueline Benn

Edited by
Jacqueline Thompson, www.EQUUS101.com
Emily Blackburn

*